UNDERSTANDING THE DREAMS YOU DREAM

VOLUME II

EVERY DREAMER'S HANDBOOK

IRA L. MILLIGAN

Treasure House

An Imprint of

Destiny Image® Publishers, Inc.
P.O. Box 310
Shippensburg, PA 17257-0310

"For where your treasure is,
there will your heart be also." Matthew 6:21

ISBN 0-7684-3030-5
(Previously published under ISBN 0-7392-0207-3 by Servant Ministries, Inc.)

For Worldwide Distribution
Printed in the U.S.A.

9 10 11 12 13 14 / 10 09 08 07 06

This book and all other Destiny Image, Revival Press, MercyPlace, Fresh Bread, Destiny Image Fiction, and Treasure House books are available at Christian bookstores and distributors worldwide.

For a U.S. bookstore nearest you, call **1-800-722-6774**.
For more information on foreign distributors, call **717-532-3040**.
Or reach us on the Internet: **www.destinyimage.com**

Dedication

This book is dedicated to my brother Alvin, who first provoked my interest in writing. Some revelations in this book were given directly to him by his loving, heavenly Father, and passed on to me in one of our many discussions about the Word of God.

Acknowledgments

I wish to express my heartfelt thanks to those precious saints of God who have supported my wife and me with their prayers and substance, allowing us to give ourselves wholly to prayer and to the ministry of the Word. Without them, this book would not exist. I am eternally grateful for them.

I'm especially indebted to Vicki Camp and Jimmy Skinner for their help in proofreading the manuscript.

I would also like to thank each dreamer who sent their dreams and gave me permission to use them. Their contributions have greatly enriched this book.

Contents

Introduction

DREAMS REMAIN ONE OF THE MOST CONTROVERSIAL SUBJECTS in the church today. Some people simply say, "I never dream." Others emphatically state, "I never pay attention to dreams. They're nonsense. They come from eating too much pizza." Yet others seem to obtain valuable insight from meditating upon their dreams. They claim dreams are a dependable source of guidance and information for their lives. Which group is right? Should we pay attention to dreams, or simply ignore them as just so much junk mail?

The Bible gives us a direct answer to this question: "And it shall come to pass in the last days, saith God, I will pour out of My Spirit upon all flesh: and...your old men shall dream dreams" (Acts 2:17). That's God's promise—and by the way, one does not have to be an old man to dream. Young men dream too! God is talking about our "old man," as in our carnal nature. At the present time, He is indiscriminately pouring out His Spirit upon young and old alike. He uses dreams to encourage His children and direct them in their walk with Him, and He uses them to warn sinners to repent. The Scriptures contain numerous dreams; if they were removed, a large portion of the Bible would be missing. Without them, a large measure of God's guidance for the Church is also missing (including personal instructions for every individual). Everyone has the ability to dream, so no one should be without God's personal guidance. God has used dreams to communicate with His people from the beginning. He doesn't change, so He has not changed, and will not change the way He speaks to us. Although dreams are only one of the many ways that He speaks, they are certainly a legitimate source of divine information and knowledge.

Dreams are elusive. Everyone has them, but they're like the morning fog; they quickly evaporate. If we do not make a deliberate effort to capture them, they simply vanish. By the time we get our morning coffee, they're usually forgotten. Very few are vivid enough to automatically burn themselves into our consciousness.

For those who don't seem to dream at all, my advice is first ask God for dreams, and then pay close attention each morning for His answer. I met one man who claimed he didn't dream; but after asking for dreams, he received *ten* in just three weeks. In the Bible, James said we receive not because we ask not, and Paul admonished us to seek God's gifts (see Jas. 4:2; 1 Cor. 14:1). Dreams are indeed a gift from God. They are one of His ways of imparting a "word of wisdom" and a "word of knowledge" to us (see 1 Cor. 12:8). In addition to wisdom and knowledge, some dreams are prophetic—inspired by and received directly from the spirit of prophecy. These messages should be considered as "thus saith the Lord."

We should no more ignore our dreams than our mail. Certainly all of our mail is not valuable, but wouldn't it be foolish to throw it all out unopened just because in the past some of it proved to be junk mail?

Sometimes, dream interpretation can be heavy stuff, so I've written this book in a conversational style interlaced with a little humor to lighten it up a bit. I have already covered the basic rules for proper dream interpretation in my previous book, *Understanding the Dreams You Dream*, including a comprehensive symbol dictionary. This book complements the former book's dictionary by teaching the *language* of dreams. It reveals much more than just what symbols mean; it also explains why they mean what they mean. I trust that God will be glorified and the reader blessed by the information contained herein. Thanks be to God for His unspeakable gift!

Chapter One

The Dreamer's Dilemma

Have you ever dreamed that you won the lottery, but after waking, you couldn't remember the winning numbers? Frustrating! Equally frustrating is dreaming of looking for a specific house or room number, and although you wake up remembering the number, you have no idea what it means. Have you ever dreamed of getting on an elevator and going to the ninth floor? This may mean good things are ahead. But if you've dreamed of getting off on the tenth floor, it could be bad news! Although numbers are rather common in dreams, most books about dreams just ignore them. This one doesn't. Chapters Two through Six provide an in-depth study on numbers, while the remaining chapters focus on the meanings of colors, locations, animals, vehicles, metal, trades, and several other categories. This book concludes listing important rules to follow when interpreting dreams and some commonly asked questions.

A Number of Ways to Interpret Symbols

Many dream symbols are relatively easy to interpret because they have a limited number of applications. For instance, an apple in a dream can represent *sin*, as when Eve ate of the forbidden fruit, or it can portray *appreciation*, as when a child gives an apple to his teacher. A sour apple may refer to a person with a *bad disposition*, and a big apple may even represent *New York City*, because it's well known as "The Big Apple."

Dreaming about a basket of apples may signify that one is *fruitful*, bringing forth "the fruit of the Spirit," or the apples may refer to *wise counsel*, as in Proverbs 25:11: "A word fitly spoken is like apples of gold in pictures of silver." Dreaming of a rotten apple may mean that one is keeping bad company, as in, "One rotten apple spoils the whole barrel," or dreaming about stealing a bright red apple may refer to one's natural passion for forbidden fruit. But there's certainly a limit to the various possible meanings an apple can convey; however, this limitation does not apply to numbers, the subject we will first examine in this book. Numbers are virtually unlimited in their applications. They can mean almost anything.

It is not uncommon for dreams to include numbers within their content. Numbers are the very highest form of symbolism; therefore, their meanings are seldom understood. The number *one* has the potential of meaning anything from one person to one city to one nation to one universe! It has an unlimited number of meanings, or at least as many as there are things in existence! Because there are endless meanings for every number, of necessity everyone must use a common reference before numbers can be considered useful in dreams. God has provided just such a reference tool for us—the Bible.

But before discussing the actual meanings of individual numbers, we need to examine how symbols obtain their various meanings in the first place.

How Symbols Acquire Their Meanings

THERE ARE FOUR PRIMARY WAYS that symbols acquire specific meanings. One, and probably the most common way, is by the symbol's *inherent character*. Because a symbol's basic characteristics are the same the world over, this is sometimes referred to as a symbol's *universal* meaning. For instance, in the Bible, God used innocent lambs to represent His children, and merciless wolves to describe their enemies. The descriptive nature, or character, of these two animals clearly illustrates what they're depicting. Another example is the inherent characteristics of a motorcyclist. Motorcyclists often symbolize pride and rebellion because of the attitude many of them exhibit. *Individuality*, or even *loner*, are other possible meanings, because cycles are usually ridden alone. Besides the rider's attitude, two characteristics of the machine itself are speed and agility. Noise is another. When one dreams of a motorcycle, the dream's content usually indicates which meaning applies.

Another way a symbol may obtain a specific meaning is through a dreamer's *personal experience*. An object, animal, person, color, or location may mean something to one person that would not mean the same to another. If you've ever ridden a motorcycle and had an accident, motorcycles may mean sudden calamity to you! Another, more probable example is your pet dog or cat; either one may denote something precious to you because of your love for it. In another case, someone unfamiliar with your child-hood home or toys would not see them the same way that you do. The Bible has an interesting precedent for personal experience influencing spiritual perception:

> *And out of the ground the Lord God formed every beast of the field, and every fowl of the air; and brought them unto Adam to see what he would call them: and whatsoever Adam called every living creature, that was the name thereof* (Genesis 2:19).

In other words, God speaks our language. Often the way we perceive something carries over into our dreams, even when our perception is less than perfect.

A third way symbols acquire meaning is through *society*. Our *culture* may influence our perception of certain symbols and give them special meaning. If someone says that a disgruntled employee "has gone postal," most Americans know exactly what he means. But say that to an assembly in East Africa and your interpreter will peer at you sideways with a funny look on his face! Likewise, there are several sayings and parables in the Bible that people from Western societies find difficult to interpret. Occasionally, even colloquialisms are used in Scripture.

If one is unaware of a certain Jewish saying, he could get the wrong impression of Jesus when reading the following Scripture passage:

> *And [Jesus] said unto another, Follow Me. But he said, Lord, **suffer me first to go and bury my father**. Jesus said unto him, Let the dead bury their dead: but go thou and preach the king-dom of God* (Luke 9:59-60, emphasis added).

Although it sounds like Jesus was being incredibly hard, that is not the case. The man's father was still alive. When the man said, "Suffer me first to go and bury my father," he actually meant, "Wait until after my father dies and I get my inheritance, *then* I'll follow You." Jesus was directly addressing this man's covetousness. He challenged him to forsake his inheritance and take up his cross. If you are trying to help someone interpret a dream and you're unaware of his cultural perception of a symbol used in it, there's no possible way that you can offer him a correct interpretation.

On the other hand, some symbols first acquire meaning in one culture and later become accepted all over the world. A prime example is a red cross. Although it has no inherent character of its own, it has come to mean *medical aid* to all nations.

And last (and by far the most important when dealing especially with numbers), a symbol acquires meaning by the way it is used in *Scripture*. By studying the various ways numbers and other objects are used in the Bible, we can see exactly what they mean in our dreams. For numbers, there's no other dependable source of information available. When a dream is from God (and many are), we can always depend upon the *"more sure word of prophecy"* to show us exactly what He means, because God does not change.

Chapter Two

Bible Numerology 101

THE BIBLE IS THE ONLY LEGITIMATE SOURCE of knowledge for the symbolic meaning of numbers. Therefore, our discussion is based solely upon the Word of God. God uses numbers in dreams identically to the way He uses them in Scripture. Subsequently, there is a double blessing in learning about numbers; we can understand both our dreams *and* the Bible more fully. Once we have mastered the message of our dreams, many passages in the Bible suddenly take on a completely new meaning.

Beginning in the very first book of the Bible, Genesis, even a casual reader soon discovers that it is filled with numbers. God numbers almost everything, and when He counts, He seldom does it for the same reason we do. His numbers reveal more than just quantity! For instance, let's take a look at the number *seven* in Scripture.

Number Seven—Complete

BECAUSE GOD *COMPLETED ALL* HIS WORK and *finished* it on the seventh day of creation, we can reasonably deduct that seven means "complete" (see Gen. 2:1-2). In fact, most Bible scholars agree that it means "complete," "finished," or "all." And because God rested after He finished, it can also mean "rest." In the same way, the other six days of creation reveal the meanings of numbers *one* through *six*.

Number One—Beginning

UNDERSTANDABLY, THE VERY FIRST NUMBER mentioned in Genesis is *one*, and God defines it at the same time He introduces it. "In the beginning...[was] the first day" (see Gen. 1:1-5). Thus we can see that the symbolic meaning for *one* is "beginning." Another meaning is "first," as we might say, "God is number one in my book!" By this we mean that He comes first; He's the best, most important, etc. One thing is for certain, God is number one in every sense of the word! Of course, in the natural use of the word, *one* can also mean "singular," as in "one God."

Number Two—Divide or Judge

NEXT, THE BIBLE DEFINES the number *two*. In the second day God divided the waters that were under the firmament from the waters above the firmament (see Gen. 1:6-8). It doesn't take a rocket scientist to glean from this passage that *two* means "divide." At the final judgment, God will divide the sheep from the goats (see Mt. 25:32). So, by extension, *two* means "to judge," "to discern," or "to set apart." In the same way, since the Bible requires a minimum of two witnesses before judgment can be rendered, occasionally "witness" is an acceptable meaning (see Deut. 17:6). In the Bible, the concept of dividing and judging are so closely interwoven that you seldom see one without the other.

One of the clearest examples of this is found in First Kings. When Solomon was first crowned king and was at Gibeon offering sacrifices, he had a dream in which he asked God for wisdom to govern Israel properly. After he returned to Jerusalem, two harlots were brought before him for judgment. Both had delivered a child, but one had accidentally killed her own baby and was claiming the living baby as her own:

> And the king said, Bring me a sword....And the king said, **Divide** the living child in two, and give half to the one, and half to the other. Then spake the woman whose the living child was unto the king, for her bowels yearned upon her son, and she said, O my lord, give her the living child, and in no wise slay it. But the other said, Let it be neither mine nor thine, but **divide** it. Then the king answered and said, Give her the living

*child, and in no wise slay it: she is the mother thereof. And all
Israel heard of the judgment which the king had **judged**; and
they feared the king: for they saw that the wisdom of God was in
him, to do **judgment*** (1 Kings 3:24-28, emphasis added).

One other thought should be considered here. These women
each accused the other—one justly, the other fraudulently. Likewise, in court, the alleged perpetrator of a crime is called, "the
accused." Thus, by extension, "to be judgmental" or "to accuse" is
another meaning for *two*.

Number Three—Conform

ALTHOUGH THE MEANING for the number *three* may not be as easily discerned by reading the Book of Genesis, additional study
of the Scripture reveals the meaning of *three* as "conform." In the
third day God caused the dry land (ashamed land, Heb.) to appear
by dividing the waters (see Gen. 1:9). The dry, ashamed land corresponds to our repentance and confession as we come out of sin
into conformity to God's image. Paul said that we are "predes-
tin[ed] to be conformed to the image of His Son" (Rom. 8:29b),
even as Christ Himself was conformed to the express "image of the
invisible God" (Col. 1:15b). So we should be conformed in all
three areas of our being—spirit, soul, and body. A few more words
conveying this same concept are "obey," "imitate," and "copy."

Number Four—Rule or Reign

THE NUMBER *FOUR* is a little easier to define. In the fourth day of
creation God made "two great lights"—the sun and moon (see
Gen. 1:16). These were made specifically to "rule" the day and
night. From this, we can deduct that *four* means "rule." Although
the primary meaning of *four* is "rule" or "reign," by extension its
meaning may include the ruler's subjects. Thus, the symbolism of
four may include certain aspects of the world, as in the four cor-
ners of the world, or the four winds of the earth (see Rev. 7:1).
One word used extensively in Scripture which embodies both ruler
and subject is *kingdom*. Also, by implication, *dominion* or *dominance*
is sometimes the symbolic thought contained in the number *four*.

Number Five—Serve

A S WITH THE NUMBER *THREE*, it's a little more difficult to discover the meaning of number *five* from the record of creation than it is for numbers *one*, *two*, and *four*. The fifth day was the first day that living creatures were made. All living things were made for God's pleasure, to serve Him, so *five* means "service" or "works." When God challenged Job, He asked him, "Will the unicorn be willing to *serve* thee?....or will he harrow the valleys after thee?" (Job 39:9-10, emphasis added) Of course, the answer is no! He works for God, and only God!

This leads to a unique understanding of why God tells us that if we don't pay our tithe, we must add a fifth part to it. If we withhold God's just due, we will go into bondage (debt); and the borrower *serves* the lender (see Lev. 27:31; Prov. 22:7)! Hence, *five* means "serve." We all serve something (or someone); the question is what or who? Are we serving a good master, or laboring for a bad one? Often the choice is ours.

While we're talking about serving, by implication, *five* can also refer to "law." The Jews tried to become righteous through their own works by obeying the Law. So, *five* also points to legalism, or one who is legalistic. According to Paul, the Law brought bondage, so five can also symbolize various addictions like alcoholism and gambling. And as we previously mentioned, bondage may include debt. The Bible also identifies another type of bondage—fear (see Heb. 2:15).

Number Six—Image

T HE SIXTH DAY ALSO UNVEILS the Creator's meaning for the number of that day. On that day, God made man in His own *image* (see Gen. 1:27). Although *six* has often been called "the number of man," that definition unjustly limits it. The meaning of *six* includes more than just "man." For instance, "Nebuchadnezzar the king made an *image* of gold, whose height was threescore [sixty] cubits, and the breadth thereof six cubits" (Dan. 3:1a, emphasis added). As the sixty-cubit high and six-cubic wide idol in this verse shows, *six* can refer to something besides man. Even though idols are images, they aren't necessarily made like men who have been made after God's own image. Instead, they usually portray demons (see Dan. 3:1; 1 Cor. 10:19-20). But being images, the number *six* fits them well. Later, after we discuss *ten* and *one hundred*, we will explore the meaning of John's infamous 666 that we've heard so much about.

Just how useful understanding numbers can be is shown in a dream that a pastor recently related to me. He dreamed he was defending himself with what he thought was a .36-caliber pistol. But after he shot and wounded his opponent, he realized that his pistol wasn't a .36-caliber after all, but rather it was a .32-caliber. The meaning? This pastor thought he was conformed to Christ's image (36), but God was showing him that he had a judgmental attitude instead. There's quite a stretch between the two. The image Christ portrayed was love. Jesus said He didn't come to judge the world, but to save it.

So there you have it. Seven days—seven numbers explained, but what about *eight* and *nine*? Again, the Bible has the answers. But before we look for them, we need to examine another concept about symbols—the difference between direct and implied meanings.

Roots or Branches

THERE IS A BASIC INTERPRETATION for each symbol. These basic interpretations are comparable to tree roots. In the same way that *roots* produce plants with *branches*, each root meaning branches out and produces additional meanings through implication. In other words, branch meanings are implied meanings. To further complicate things, sometimes roots branch out in several different directions. Also, in some cases, even the branches produce branches. *Two* is a prime example. First, the root meaning for *two* is "divide." By implication, *divide* means "to judge." But to judge properly, one must have at least two witnesses. Subsequently, one branch of *judge* is "witness." Thus, by extension, *two* also means "witness." In the same way, it may even include the verdict!

If we don't search deep enough and uncover the roots, we may mistake a branch for a root, which sooner or later will lead to mis-interpretation. Then, when we encounter the actual root, we will be stumped for an answer (pun intended). If we don't search and find the root meaning, we *will* misinterpret some symbols. But once we understand roots, the implied meanings are relatively easy to see and understand. We find this principal in the common, but somewhat mistaken, meaning for the number *eight*.

Number Eight—Put Off

Genesis 17:12 probably reveals the correct meaning for *eight* better than any other verse in the Bible. In it God tells Abraham, "He that is eight days old shall be circumcised among you...." Paul explains the meaning of circumcision:

*In whom also ye are circumcised with the circumcision made without hands, in **putting off** the body of the sins of the flesh by the circumcision of Christ* (Colossians 2:11, emphasis added).

In other words, the symbolic meaning for *circumcision* and the meaning for number *eight* are the same. On the eighth day we are to "put off" our "old man." Therefore, we see that the inference here is *put off*. Now, it's commonly believed that *eight* means "new beginnings," and indeed, when we put off our old man, we are born again and we start anew. But the correct root meaning for this number is "put off," and therefore, the implied meaning, "new beginning" won't always properly fit. When circumcising a baby on his eighth day, one can hardly say the baby is having a new beginning, but the covering of his flesh is certainly being put off just as God commanded. Later, when we study the teens, we will see even more clearly why understanding root meanings versus implied meanings is so important.

There are several other passages of Scripture that confirm that "put off" is the proper root for *eight*. One real good example is when Noah came out of the Ark on the mountains of Ararat. When the flood was over, the earth certainly had a new beginning, but Noah didn't land nor exit on the eighth year, nor the eighth month, nor even the eighth day. Rather, "the ark rested in the seventh month, on the seventeenth day of the month..." (Gen. 8:4). And then Noah emerged on the "...six hundredth and first year, in the first month, the first day of the month..." (Gen. 8:13). As we can see from the numbers used, God finished His work (the ark rested in the seventh month), and started anew (Noah emerged on the first year, first month, and first day). With God, all beginnings are new, and the number *one* covers them all!

Another Scripture to help us properly understand *eight* is Exodus 22:30. God told Moses to allow the newborn offspring of the sheep and oxen to stay with their respective mothers for seven days, but on the eighth day they were to be sacrificed unto Him. Of course, sacrificing their flesh symbolizes the circumcision of our flesh ("putting off" our old man). Another similar reference is when Moses reiterated their wilderness journey where God destroyed ("put off") the old men from among their tribes:

And the space in which we came from Kadesh-barnea, until we were come over the brook Zered, was thirty and eight years; until all the generation of the men of war were wasted out from among the host... (Deuteronomy 2:14).

It wasn't until they were conformed to His will, and the old men were put off ("wasted out") in the wilderness, that they were allowed to go in and possess their inheritance.

Number Nine—Fruit or Harvest

THE NUMBER *NINE* MEANS "fruit" or "harvest," and its meaning is made all the more interesting because of the age of Noah's grandfather Methuselah. He lived longer than anyone else in the Bible: "And all the days of Methuselah were nine hundred sixty and nine years: and he died" (Gen. 5:27).

Some translators say that his name means, "when he is gone it [the flood] shall come." Others say it means, "they died." Either way, as Hosea said many centuries later, "Also, O Judah, [God] hath set an harvest for thee..." (Hosea 6:11). Methuselah's age at death signaled the beginning of God's first harvest of judgment upon the earth. Nine hundred sixty-nine reveals the earth's harvest was ripe; the image and fruit was rotten and rejected. The first harvest was by water; the second will be by fire:

And another angel came out of the temple, crying with a loud voice to him that sat on the cloud, Thrust in thy sickle, and reap: for the time is come for thee to reap; for the harvest of the earth is ripe (Revelation 14:15).

Although in both of the aforementioned harvests the earth is cursed, *nine* can also signify blessings. In fact, understanding the symbolic meaning of *nine* gives new and added dimension to one of Jesus' most moving parables:

> *What man of you, having an hundred sheep, if he lose one of them, doth not leave the ninety and nine in the wilderness, and go after that which is lost, until he find it?...likewise joy shall be in heaven over one sinner that repenteth, more than over ninety and nine just persons, which need no repentance* (Luke 15:4,7).

It's easy to see that "ninety and nine" refers to God's harvest of souls. And then later, when Jesus healed the ten lepers, He asked: "Were there not ten cleansed? but where are the nine?" (Lk. 17:17b) Jesus was asking, "Where is My harvest of thanksgiving?" The fruit of *all* their lips should have been giving thanks to His name (see Heb. 13:15)!

We have now covered the basics. *One* is "beginning"; *two* is to "divide" or "judge"; *three* is "conform"; *four* is to "rule" or "reign" (over a subject); *five* is to "serve" or "work"; *six* is "image"; *seven* is "complete"; *eight* is to "put off"; and *nine* is "fruit" or "harvest." When Moses gave the Law to the Israelites, he advised them to be circumspect, that is, to look around at the complete picture. When interpreting dreams, we should follow Moses' advice and not be narrow-minded! Sometimes there are slight overlaps in meanings. As we continue our study, we'll learn that numbers like *seven* and *thousand* come close to meaning the same thing at times; likewise, *five* and *eighteen* will have the same meaning in some cases. We've learned how important understanding roots are. When we studied the numbers *two* and *eight*, we also discovered that a root may produce a branch—implied meaning. Whether we use the root or the branch always depends upon the application. Once we've mastered the root meanings, we can safely move on to the implications and additions that they allow.

There is another minor point that we need to consider before we move on to more advanced numbers. When interpreting any symbol, there is always the possibility that it's not used as a symbol at all, but rather it simply means what it says (or is). When Joseph interpreted Pharaoh's dreams about seven cows eating seven other cows, seven cows meant seven years rather than "complete," and earlier, when he interpreted the butler and baker's dreams, the three branches and baskets meant three days (see Gen. 41:26; 40:12,18). At other times (and quite often in Scripture), the meaning is dual, and can correctly be seen in its natural application as well as with symbolic meaning. A prime example is, "God is one!" He is indeed singular; there is only one God. But also, He is number one—the first; the beginning; the best; the most important; and He certainly should be counted as number one by all.

Chapter Three

Multiplied Multiples

"**M**ULTIPLES, MULTIPLES IN THE VALLEY of decision..." Oops! That's supposed to be, "Multitudes, multitudes in the valley of decision: for the day of the Lord is near in the valley of decision" (Joel 3:14). But it's close, anyway. After all, there are a multitude of decisions to make when God starts using numbers in dreams. In fact, we're now getting into the *really* interesting numbers—numbers like *ten*, *twenty*, *thirty*, or even *hundreds* and *thousands*. And when God puts dollar signs in front of them, they get even more interesting! Have you ever dreamed that you won a sweepstake? It'll get your attention; that's for sure. We'll discuss just such a dream toward the end of this chapter.

Growing a Garden

JUST AS WE STUDIED the base numbers individually, we also need to examine the numbers that contain multiple digits one at a time. As we progressed from one digit to another in the last chapter, you may have guessed that the meaning of each number in some way relates to the one preceding or following it; if so, you were right—it does. Jesus taught that His Kingdom was a lot like growing a garden:

> *...The kingdom of God is as if a man should scatter seed on the ground, and should sleep by night and rise by day, and the seed should sprout and grow, he himself does not know how. For the earth yields crops by itself: first the blade, then the head, after that the full grain in the head. But when the grain ripens,*

immediately he puts in the sickle, because the harvest has come (Mark 4:26-29, NKJ).

One is like a seed. We start our garden with a seed, and through the growth process, we obtain the harvest.

There are nine numbered steps from planting to harvest. Count them as I name them off. A seed is singular, and of utmost importance. Our garden *begins* when the seed is planted in fertile soil. The seed then *divides* itself and sends a root downward, and a shoot upward. A leaf breaks though the surface and *conforms* itself in every way to its parent plant. It struggles to survive and *conquer* drought, heat, insects—and if it prevails, it goes to *work* producing blooms, buds, etc. to form other seed to *replicate* itself. After the fruit or seed forms, it *completely* ripens and finally, the husk, shell, or peeling is *put off* and the *fruit is harvested*. Once harvested, the fruit is appraised for its quality and *weighed* or *measured* for its quantity.

Number Ten—Weighed in the Balances

APPRAISING AND WEIGHING the fruit is the tenth step, and it corresponds to the number *ten*. *Ten* means to "weigh" or "measure" for the specific purpose of *accepting* or *rejecting* that which is weighed. During this process, most Christians simply say they are being tried. In his letter to the church in Smyrna, John admonished:

> *Fear none of those things which thou shalt suffer: behold, the devil shall cast some of you into prison, that ye may be **tried**; and ye shall have tribulation **ten** days: be thou faithful unto death, and I will give thee a crown of life* (Revelation 2:10, emphasis added).

So we see that dreaming of getting off an elevator on the tenth floor may be a warning that we are about to enter into a trial.

As we mentioned in the first chapter, when we dream of taking an elevator ride, getting off on the ninth floor is fine, but we really don't want to get off on the tenth! If we dream that, we need to start praying Jesus' model prayer: "Our Father which art in heaven, Hallowed be Thy name. Thy kingdom come. Thy will be done....And lead us not into temptation, but deliver us..." (Mt. 6:9b-10,13). On the other hand, if we dream of getting off on the ninth floor in our local court house, and the ninth floor happens to be where the judge's office is, then *nine* simply means *nine*; and the message of the dream is written on the office door!

Opposite Interpretations

NOW THAT BRINGS UP ANOTHER interesting point. If one is tried and passes the test, the outcome is good. But what if one fails? If either quality or quantity are lacking in someone as he is being "weighed" or "measured," the results will be disappointing. When interpreting symbols, it's important to recognize this concept: *Almost every symbol can be interpreted two different ways–either negative or positive.* Therefore, it's possible for each ordinary symbol to have a dual meaning. However, numbers are unique. For instance, how can "beginning" be positive or negative? Positives and negatives are opposites. The opposite of beginning is ending. Ending up in Heaven is not a negative! As we continue our study, we'll see that God has provided opposites for the base numbers in a very special way. In fact, they're not always opposites; sometimes they're actually *results*. But for now, let's return to the subject of double digits.

Two Times Ten

WHEN WE TAKE A BASE NUMBER (one through nine), and multiply it by ten, we are weighing or measuring it to determine whether to accept or reject it. For example, two times ten equals twenty. *Twenty* means to "divide" or "judge" something, and in the process determine whether to "accept" or "reject" it. When God numbered Israel, He counted only those who were "twenty years old and upward" (see Num. 1:3). Unless God accepts you when He judges you, He will not count you as His own. From this example it's not difficult to see that *twenty* can mean "holy" (separated unto God and accepted by Him). Or, it can mean "unholy" (weighed in the balances and found wanting!). As always, the surrounding context within the dream determines whether the interpretation is positive or negative.

John saw four and twenty elders seated around God's throne:

And round about the throne were four and twenty seats: and upon the seats I saw four and twenty elders sitting, clothed in white raiment; and they had on their heads crowns of gold (Revelation 4:4).

Seats indicate positions of authority, and crowns refer to recognized authorities. Likewise, *four* means to "rule." *Twenty* means "holy," if one is accepted, which these obviously are, because they are wearing white raiment, which signifies righteousness. These men represent far more than just 24 elders. They stand for all of God's holy, righteous, ruling elders who are even now ministering around His throne. At the same time, John saw four beasts that represent the apostles, prophets, evangelists and pastor-teachers— but that's another book.

Thirty

THE NEXT NUMBER, *thirty* (three times ten) means "acceptably conformed," or if one is conformed to this world, "unacceptably conformed," but "conformed," nonetheless (see Rom. 12:2). The best example of God's use of this number is Jesus' age when He began His ministry—*thirty*. In the Old Testament, a Levite had to be thirty years old before he could become a priest or serve in the tabernacle. And to legitimately serve Christ, we must be conformed to His image (see Num. 4:3; Rom. 8:29).

Joseph is another minister who was thirty before he took office (see Gen. 41:46). Until then, "the word of the Lord tried him" (Ps. 105:19b). If he had failed God's tests and conformed to the wishes of Potiphar's wife, the story would have ended entirely different (see Gen. 39:7-8). David was another who was thirty before he was promoted: "David was thirty years old when he began to reign, and he reigned forty years" (2 Sam. 5:4). And while we're discussing David, notice the length of his reign—forty years.

Forty

MANY OF THE OLD TESTAMENT KINGS ruled forty years. Why? *Forty* means "acceptable" or "unacceptable rule," or rule that has been determined to be good or evil. *Four* means "rule," and four times ten equals acceptable or unacceptable dominion. God revealed the sovereignty of His rule in the days of Noah when He sent forty days of rain and destroyed the world. At another time, He gave Nineveh forty days to straighten up. Likewise, Jesus took dominion and ruled over both His flesh and the devil when He completed His forty-day fast.

Another example of forty depicting rule, or dominion, is revealed in the biblical story of Elisha (see 2 Kings 2:23-24). Elisha cursed a group of young people who were mocking him. Afterward, two she bears came out of the woods and executed God's judgment by mauling forty-two of them. The bears represent the curse, forty portrays dominion, and two implies judgment.

Fifty

I N SCRIPTURE, *fifty* usually relates to ministry, as *thirty* does, but with a different view. Concerning the Levitical priesthood, Moses wrote:

> *From thirty years old and upward until fifty years old shalt thou number them; all that enter in to perform the service, to do the work in the tabernacle of the congregation* (Numbers 4:23).

Thirty indicates whether a minister's *character* is conformed to Christ's, and *fifty* considers whether his *service* is. Notice the *five* and *fifty* in the following Scripture about Solomon's work force: "These were the chief of the officers that were over Solomon's work, five hundred and fifty..." (1 Kings 9:23). Also, when Jesus went to feed the five thousand, "...He said to His disciples, Make them sit down by fifties in a company" (Lk. 9:14). It's very important to get a passing grade on God's report card. Our works are regularly checked and graded. Solomon said, "For God shall bring every work into judgment, with every secret thing, whether it be good, or whether it be evil" (Eccles. 12:14).

Sixty

N OW *SIXTY* IS QUITE INTRIGUING. It's different! Because *six* means "image," *sixty* is the measure of our *image*. Our flesh is created in the image of God, and our spirit is created in His likeness. The nature of our flesh is totally unacceptable, while our spirit is ready and willing to serve God. Paul said, "...in me [that is, in my flesh] dwelleth no good thing" (Rom. 7:18a). Also, "the carnal mind is enmity against God: for it is not subject to the law of God, neither indeed can be" (Rom. 8:7). For this reason, the number *sixty* is seldom used in a positive sense in relation to mankind because it refers more to the outward image than to the inward likeness. As a whole, mankind does not have an acceptable image. Very few people have earned enough of God's approval so that He can use the number *sixty* in a positive way when referring to them. Enoch was one of the few:

> *And all the days of Enoch were three hundred sixty and five years: and Enoch walked with God: and he was not; for God took him* (Genesis 5:23-24).

(We will investigate the full meaning of Enoch's age later when we discuss hundreds.)

A pastor had this dream:

> I was in high school, trying out for the basketball team. The coach gave me three blue bowls and told me to take the players outside and line them up. I put out the bowls and we walked *exactly* sixty yards away from them. The coach said, "Go," and we started running for a bowl. The ones who raced to the bowls first got to try out for the team.

The interesting thing about this dream is the emphasis placed upon the exact distance of "sixty yards," which indicates a conformed image (one yard is three feet). The finish line was three blue bowls, which depicts a conformed, heavenly vessel. In this dream, God was reminding this pastor that all his efforts were to be directed toward being conformed to the express image of Jesus Christ.

Seventy

SEVENTY MEANS "COMPLETELY ACCEPTED" (or "completely rejected," as the case may be). Jesus used this number when He taught about forgiveness:

> *Then came Peter to Him, and said, Lord, how oft shall my brother sin against me, and I forgive him? till seven times? Jesus saith unto him, I say not unto thee, Until seven times: but, Until seventy times seven* (Matthew 18:21-22).

Peter's question conveys our carnal idea of forgiveness. *Seven* means "complete," and we think we have forgiven when we have completely released someone from his or her indebtedness to us. But Jesus teaches that we must go further. It's not enough to just forgive them; we must also completely accept them! Our concept is, "I'll forgive you this time, but I'm not going to let you get close enough to harm me again." Admittedly, it's not very wise to be like Abner and die, "as a fool dieth" (2 Sam. 3:33b), but in essence, Jesus said, "If you want Me to accept you after I've forgiven you, you also have to accept them." That's the *real* meaning of *seventy times seven* used here; the meaning is not the multiplied product of four hundred ninety.

For those who may have a problem believing that Jesus' reply to Peter's question was a parable, consider Matthew 13:34, "All these things spake Jesus unto the multitude in parables; and without a parable spake He not unto them." When we treat symbols literally instead of as parables, which they truly are, we completely miss what God is trying to tell us.

As we said, *seventy* can be negative too. One example found in the Bible is where, "seventy men of the ancients of the house of Israel" (Ezek. 8:11) were burning incense to other gods, and God asked Ezekiel:

> ...*Son of man, hast thou seen what the ancients of the house of Israel do in the dark, every man in the chambers of his imagery? for they say, The Lord seeth us not; the Lord hath forsaken the earth* (Ezekiel 8:12).

The context shows that God was completely rejecting Israel at that time because of their evil worship. Noah's father is another good example. His was the last generation before the flood: "And all the days of Lamech were seven hundred seventy and seven years: and he died" (Gen. 5:31). It sounds like God was saying, "That's all, folks"; doesn't it?

Eighty

*E*IGHTY IS WELL KNOWN as the age of Moses when God sent him to Pharaoh to deliver Israel (see Ex. 7:7). Also, Caleb was *eighty-five* when he conquered Mount Hebron (see Josh. 14:10). Although their accomplishments at that age were impressive, the meaning of their age makes them even more impressive. These men had *acceptably put off the flesh* to the point that God could be glorified through them. On the other hand, *eighty* can also be used in a negative sense:

> *And Methuselah lived an hundred **eighty** and seven years, and begat Lamech: and Methuselah lived after he begat Lamech seven hundred **eighty** and two years, and begat sons and daughters....And Lamech lived an hundred **eighty** and two years, and begat* [Noah] (Genesis 5:25-26,28, emphasis added).

Methuselah was Noah's grandfather, and Lamech was his dad. The ages of these two men epitomize their generations—rejected of God. Of their generations God said:

> *The earth also was corrupt before God, and the earth was filled with violence. And God looked upon the earth, and, behold, it was corrupt; for all flesh had corrupted his way upon the earth. And God said unto Noah, The end of all flesh is come before Me; for the earth is filled with violence through them; and, behold, I will destroy them with the earth* (Genesis 6:11-13).

And He did just that!

Ninety

NINETY MEANS the fruit has been inspected! Probably the best known passage in the Old Testament using *ninety* is found in Genesis:

> *And when Abram was ninety years old and nine, the Lord appeared to Abram, and said unto him, I am the Almighty God; walk before Me, and be thou perfect....And I will make thee exceeding fruitful, and I will make nations of thee, and kings shall come out of thee* (Genesis 17:1,6).

Appropriately enough, this visitation happened immediately before God fulfilled His promise to Abraham. Abraham was one hundred years old when Isaac was born. Of course, the fruit that God inspected and accepted was Abraham's faith, one of the nine fruits of the Spirit. And while we are on *ninety*, remember the "ninety and nine sheep" we discussed earlier when we were studying the number *nine*?

> *I say unto you, that likewise joy shall be in heaven over one sinner that repenteth, more than over ninety and nine just persons, which need no repentance* (Luke 15:7).

Since they didn't need repentance, they were certainly accepted, wouldn't you say?

A "Winning" Dream

N OW, LET'S LOOK at an actual dream that contains numbers. In the beginning of this chapter, I asked whether you've ever dreamed that you won the sweepstakes. Well, I have, more than once. Regretfully, so far it has only been in my dreams. Here is one of those dreams:

> The phone rang and my wife answered it. I could hear someone telling her that I had won $26,876. (When I awoke, I wasn't sure about the "76.") She asked whoever it was if he wanted to talk to me, and he said no, she was to just tell me that I had won.

Some background information might be helpful before attempting an interpretation. At this point in my life, I was doing a lot of self-examination and soul-searching and was questioning God concerning my "right standing" with Him. With this thought in mind, let's take a look at the dream. First, the indirect phone call (my wife answering and receiving the message instead of me) is God answering my questions through my dream. My wife represents my carnal mind, which receives the dream and passes the message on to my conscious mind as I awake. As I consciously pray and meditate upon the dream, I perceive the interpretation, which in turn edifies my spirit. Second, winning something like a lottery or sweepstakes usually refers to being unexpectedly favored and blessed. Finally, the interpretation of the number 26,800 is: *Twenty-six thousand* means the image has been judged as mature and acceptable. (How do I know that it's accepted? I won, remember?) *Eight hundred* means that the old man (carnal nature) has been fully put off. If the number *seventy-six* was the correct amount (I wasn't sure that I remembered the number correctly when I awoke), it confirms that the image was not only accepted, but was also complete (mature). So God was reassuring me during this time of self-doubt and self-examination that I was indeed "...accepted in the beloved" (Eph. 1:6).

The Fullness of Hundred

I 'M SURE YOU HAVE NOTICED that I interpreted the number *eight hundred* as *"fully* put off." Like *ten, hundred* is also a unit of measure. It means "fullness." Now that we know the base numbers, and the concept of measurement, it's easy to understand the meaning of the hundreds: fully begun (100), fully judged (200), fully conformed (300), etc.

In Judges 7:2-7, God wouldn't allow Gideon to fight for Him until He had first reduced Gideon's army to three hundred men. Why? Gideon had to fully conform to God's plan before He would use him. With this concept in mind, look again at Enoch's age—three hundred sixty-five (see Gen. 5:23). *Three hundred* means that he was fully conformed. *Sixty* means that *what* he was conformed to was God's immaculate, though invisible, image (and God's image *is* acceptable!), and *five* refers to Enoch's service. So Enoch's age revealed that *God fully accepted Enoch's person and his works.* When God fully accepts the Church, He'll take us to Heaven too!

The proper understanding of *hundred* would have saved many ministers a lot of embarrassment not too long ago. When the "prosperity move" was in its prime, the saints were promised that God would restore their offerings to them one hundred times over. One of the Scriptures used to persuade them to give was Mark 10:29-30:

> *And Jesus answered and said, Verily I say unto you, There is no man that hath left house, or brethren, or sisters, or father, or mother, or wife, or children, or lands, for My sake, and the gospel's, but he shall receive an* **hundredfold** *now in this time, houses, and brethren, and sisters, and mothers, and children, and lands, with persecutions; and in the world to come eternal life* (emphasis added).

The problem is, God will not fulfill a promise He didn't make. The Bible doesn't say God would *multiply* their return by one hundred. *Hundredfold* means "full return," not one hundred times as much. God is saying that if you give, leave, or lose something for His Kingdom's sake, in the long run you will not have lost anything because He will fully repay you. We receive back with the same measure we give, as Jesus said in Luke 6:38: "Give, and it shall be given unto you...For with the same measure that ye mete withal it shall be measured to you again." That Scripture doesn't actually mention an increase either; it says, "same measure." *Same* means "same," not more. When Isaac sowed and received an hundredfold return in Genesis 26:12, he received a *full* harvest. Even though there was a famine at the time, his crop wasn't affected. He reaped a full harvest because he sowed in obedience. Now a full harvest is certainly more than the seed planted, so notice that I'm *not* saying that God won't give you an increase; I'm just saying that *hundred-fold* doesn't mean what some endorsers of the "prosperity move" said it meant.

To fully complete our abbreviated list for hundreds: *four hundred* implies full dominion; *five hundred* indicates full service; *six hundred* portrays a full image; *seven hundred* means completely full; *eight hundred* is fully put off; and *nine hundred* refers to a full harvest.

The Maturity of Thousand

THOUSANDS ARE INTERPRETED in the same way that hundreds are. *Thousand* is a unit of measurement like *ten* and *hundred*, and refers to "maturity." So *one thousand* is the beginning of maturity, and *two thousand* is mature judgment. That's the reason Joshua told the people to stay two thousand cubits behind the priest when they went to cross the Jordan and enter Canaan. They were to use mature judgment in following their leaders (see Josh. 3:4). If the people in Waco, Texas had heeded this advice, they wouldn't have been destroyed following David Koresh.

Three thousand refers to being maturely conformed, as Paul mentions in Ephesians:

> *Till we all come in the unity of the faith, and of the knowledge of the Son of God, unto a perfect* [mature] *man, unto the measure of the stature of the fulness of Christ* (Ephesians 4:13).

Four thousand refers to mature rule, and *five thousand*, mature service. Using the same line of reasoning, *six thousand* is a mature image, *seven thousand* is simply mature, because one who is complete is mature. *Eight thousand* relates to a mature attitude toward the cross, and *nine thousand* indicates the fruit is ready for harvest.

Six Hundred Threescore and Six

NOW, BEFORE WE CONCLUDE THIS CHAPTER, what about John's infamous "666" that we mentioned earlier? First, let's examine the passage in Revelation where John talks about 666:

And I beheld another beast coming up out of the earth; and he had two horns like a lamb, and he spake as a dragon....Here is wisdom. Let him that hath understanding count the number of the beast: for it is the number of a man; and his number is Six hundred threescore and six (Revelation 13:11,18).

John identifies the beast as a man. Since we know that this is an evil man, we also know the symbolism used here is negative. Thus, the interpretation is simply this: *Six hundred* describes a *full* image, *sixty* means a *rejected* image, and *six* portrays an *image*, which John plainly declared is the image of man. So, in the same way that Christ was the express image of the invisible God, this beastly man will be the warped image of the invisible devil. He will *fully* reflect satan's *despicable image*.

Chapter Four

Numbers to Live By

IN THE PRECEDING CHAPTER we learned that *one thousand* through *nine thousand* reveals the measure of our maturity in many different areas of our lives. In the same manner, *ten thousand* through *nineteen thousand* measures things to determine their size, whether they are large or small. Even intangible things, like wisdom, might, or degree of difficulty can be measured. For instance, *ten thousand* can mean something very large, like an expansive business. It can also mean a very difficult trial—large insurmountable problems that simply won't go away, giant problems such as Israel faced when challenged by Goliath. Goliath was big trouble, but not too big for God. He defeated him through a little shepherd boy.

A Ten Thousand Dollar Dream

UNDERSTANDING DREAMS CAN HELP defeat our Goliaths, too! I own a small boat, motor, and trailer. Once, when my outboard motor wasn't running right, I asked a mechanic how much he would charge to fix it. He said the repair would cost $55 an hour and would take about two hours. Besides needing the motor repaired, I was facing a lot of other problems too. Even my ministry wasn't going very well. About a week later, before I had the motor repaired, God began dealing with me about fasting, and during that time I had this dream:

> My outboard motor needed repair so I pulled my boat to
> a new marine dealer in town. Even though the dealer was

closed, I left my boat in his driveway, which was rutted and rough. When I returned, I greeted the dealer and told him that I came to get my boat. I decided to ask him how much he would charge to repair it. I was thinking that he might be cheaper than the first mechanic who had already given me an estimate. But when I asked his price, he answered $10,000. I was aghast and informed him that the other dealer would fix it for only $110. (In my mind I was figuring two hours at $55 an hour.) After consideration, the new dealer agreed to repair it for $85.

When I awoke, I realized that God was saying that my circumstances (my unhitched boat parked on a rough driveway) wasn't going to improve without repairs. The $10,000 was the insurmountable problems that I was facing at the time: debt, sickness, low income, stalled ministry, etc. The $110 was the trial I was in—the test I had to pass. Adding up the two hours at $55 each was counting the cost and making the decision to go ahead and pay the price (do the "work" of fasting) to fix the problems. Of course, the dealer represented the Lord, who was agreeing to repair the problems if I would work at putting off the flesh by going on an acceptable fast. (*Eighty* signified putting off, and *five* indicated work, or fasting.) Thus, God confirmed what I was already feeling in my spirit—I needed to fast to overcome the enemy's opposition. (For an acceptable fast, see Isaiah chapter 58.)

Twenty Thousand

IF *TEN THOUSAND* CAN MEAN a big trial, then couldn't *twenty thousand* mean something very, very holy, or maybe a very big decision that has to be made? Consider these Scriptures:

> The chariots of God are **twenty thousand**, even thousands of angels: the Lord is among them, as in Sinai, **in the holy place** (Psalm 68:17, emphasis added).

> Or what king, going to make war against another king, sitteth not down first, and **consulteth whether he be able** with ten thousand to meet him that cometh against him with **twenty thousand**? (Luke 14:31, emphasis added)

Besides having to make a big decision, that king had better make a wise one too! And, can you also see a big trial coming in that Scripture?

Thirty Thousand

NOW, WHAT ABOUT *thirty thousand*? See if you can determine something conformed, accepted, mature, and large in the following passage:

> *So Joshua arose, and all the people of war, to go up against Ai: and Joshua chose out thirty thousand mighty men of valour, and sent them away by night* (Joshua 8:3).

In case you had difficulty, "thirty" is accepted and conformed. (Chosen shows acceptance, so *thirty* is acceptably conformed.) "Thousand mighty men" implies greatness and "men of valour" refers to maturity in battle. So Joshua accepted those who were (as Paul put it) "strong in the Lord, and in the power of His might" (Eph. 6:10b).

Forty Thousand

FORTY THOUSAND IS QUITE SIMILAR, but the emphasis isn't just on a larger kingdom; instead, it emphasizes "wise rule." This fits the Scripture above where the king needed to make a wise decision about whether or not he should go to war. Words like *skillful* and *expert* are used in conjunction with this number. The following Scripture bears this out:

> *The sons...of valiant men, men able to bear buckler and sword, and to shoot with bow, and **skilful** in war, were **four** and **forty thousand** seven hundred and threescore, that went out to the war* (1 Chronicles 5:18, emphasis added).

The additional numbers also reveal that these warriors were completely conformed to an acceptable image. Likewise, the following use of *forty thousand* reveals an extraordinary ability to wage wise warfare: "And of Asher, such as went forth to battle, expert in war, *forty thousand*" (1 Chron. 12:36, emphasis added).

And while we're studying *forty thousand*, how about the controversial, "hundred forty and four thousand" of Revelation 14:1-3? Very few understand this Scripture:

And I looked, and, lo, a Lamb stood on the mount Sion, and with Him an hundred forty and four thousand, having His Father's name written in their foreheads. And I heard a voice from heaven, as the voice of many waters, and as the voice of a great thunder: and I heard the voice of harpers harping with their harps: and they sung as it were a new song before the throne, and before the four beasts, and the elders: and no man could learn that song but the hundred and forty and four thousand, which were redeemed from the earth (Revelation 14:1-3).

It's not the count, but the meaning of the number that tells the story. These people represent all the redeemed warriors of God's Kingdom—multitudes of them! These are the leaders, God's holy and righteous apostles and prophets who rule with Him over His Kingdom.

Fifty Thousand

NOW LET'S REVIEW THE BASICS in preparation for discussing *fifty thousand*. *Five* means "service" or "work," and *fifty* reveals that our works are tried (by fire), as Paul said in First Corinthians 3:13:

Every man's work shall be made manifest: for the day shall declare it, because it shall be revealed by fire; and the fire shall try every man's work of what sort it is.

As we've seen, *ten* and *thousand* are units of measure, *ten* meaning to "test" or "weigh," and *thousand* meaning "mature." But when a number is brought to the fifth place and becomes *ten thousand* or above, the thought of largeness is always involved in the interpretation. Comparing *fifty* to *fifty thousand* is like comparing a grocery cart to an eighteen-wheeler. So if *fifty* speaks of our daily testing and fiery trials, then *fifty thousand* is talking about a mighty big fire!

In fact, *fifty thousand* falls right in line with the other numbers we've studied. Fifty indicates the quality of service, whether it's accepted or rejected, and *thousand* measures its quantity. So when God tried Israel's service, sometimes He rejected it with horrible consequences:

And [God] smote the men of Beth-shemesh, because they had looked into the ark of the Lord, even He smote of the people fifty

*thousand and threescore and ten men: and the people lament-
ed, because the Lord had smitten many of the people with a
great slaughter* (1 Samuel 6:19).

And sometimes Israel's service was excellent and thus gra-
ciously accepted by the Lord, as shown in this Scripture:

*Of Zebulun, such as went forth to battle, expert in war, with all
instruments of war, fifty thousand, which could keep rank: they
were not of double heart* (1 Chronicles 12:33).

Likewise, God's presence mightily testified of the righteous
works of those who burned their idols in the New Testament. (I
find it interesting that fire was also used along with *fifty thousand*
in this passage.):

*Many of them also which used curious arts brought their books
together, and burned them before all men: and they counted the
price of them, and found it fifty thousand pieces of silver. So
mightily grew the word of God and prevailed* (Acts 19:19-20).

Sixty Thousand

THE MEANING OF *SIXTY THOUSAND* agrees with what we've already
learned about the reverse image of God. That is, our image
just doesn't agree with God. I think it gives Him indigestion. There
are only two passages in the entire Bible where *sixty thousand* is used.
We only need to look at one of them to establish its meaning:

*And it came to pass, that in the fifth year of king Rehoboam
Shishak king of Egypt came up against Jerusalem, because they
had transgressed against the Lord, with twelve hundred chariots, and* **threescore** [sixty] **thousand** *horsemen....And he took
the fenced cities which pertained to Judah, and came to
Jerusalem. Then came Shemaiah the prophet to Rehoboam, and
to the princes of Judah, that were gathered together to Jerusalem
because of Shishak, and said unto them, Thus saith the Lord,
Ye have forsaken Me, and therefore have I also left you in the
hand of Shishak* (2 Chronicles 12:2-5, emphasis added).

God was greatly displeased with His people at this time. Israel simply did not reflect His likeness.

Seventy Thousand

WHEN KING DAVID COMMITTED the sin of pride by numbering Israel, God sent a plague and destroyed seventy thousand of David's subjects. David threw himself upon the mercy of the court, but God would not relent until His judgment was complete:

> And David said unto Gad, I am in a great strait: let me fall now into the hand of the Lord; for very great are His mercies: but let me not fall into the hand of man. So the Lord sent pestilence upon Israel: and there fell of Israel seventy thousand men. And God sent an angel unto Jerusalem to destroy it: and as he was destroying, the Lord beheld, and He repented him of the evil, and said to the angel that destroyed, It is enough, stay now thine hand... (1 Chronicles 21:13-15).

Although in this Scripture *seventy thousand* specifically relates to *complete* recompense for David's transgression, it can relate to anything where the measure is large and complete.

Eighty Thousand

THE PRINCIPLE OF THOUSANDS relating to largeness remains consistent throughout the Bible. In the following Scripture, *eighty thousand* refers to a failed attempt to bring an entire kingdom under one rule:

> And when Rehoboam came to Jerusalem, he assembled all the house of Judah with the tribe of Benjamin, one hundred and **eighty thousand** chosen men who were warriors, to fight against the house of Israel, **that he might restore the kingdom** to Rehoboam the son of Solomon (1 Kings 12:21 NKJ, emphasis added).

It was a vain attempt to fully restore the whole kingdom to Rehoboam. It was vain because God was the one who cast off his rule:

> Thus says the Lord: "You shall not go up nor fight against your brethren the children of Israel. Let every man return to his house, for this thing is from Me." Therefore they obeyed the word of the Lord, and turned back, according to the word of the Lord (1 Kings 12:24 NKJ).

Ninety Thousand

S O FAR, WE'VE BEEN ABLE to show scriptural examples for almost every number we've discussed, but regretfully, *ninety thousand* is not in the Bible. So we'll assume that the established pattern remains unchanged. If we follow the same train of thought that we've seen in the previous eight numbers, *ninety thousand* refers to a very large harvest, as will occur at the end of the world:

> *Be patient therefore, brethren, unto the coming of the Lord. Behold, the husbandman waiteth for the precious fruit of the earth, and hath long patience for it, until he receive the early and latter rain. Be ye also patient; stablish your hearts: for the coming of the Lord draweth nigh* (James 5:7-8).

A Countless Multitude

I WONDER IF GOD DECIDED not to number the harvest because it's *so* large! And if He had used *ninety thousand* in reference to it, some feebleminded person would have surely tried to restrict entrance into Heaven to just those few. Simpletons discouraging the faith of the simple. In fact, there are some people who think that only one hundred forty-four thousand will make it. However, John saw so many in Heaven that no one could count them:

> *After this I beheld, and, lo, **a great multitude, which no man could number**, of all nations, and kindreds, and people, and tongues, stood before the throne, and before the Lamb, clothed with white robes, and palms in their hands; and cried with a loud voice, saying, Salvation to our God which sitteth upon the throne, and unto the Lamb. And all the angels stood round about the throne, and about the elders and the four beasts, and fell before the throne on their faces, and worshipped God, saying, Amen: Blessing, and glory, and wisdom, and thanksgiving, and honour, and power, and might, be unto our God for ever and ever. Amen. And one of the elders answered, saying unto me, What are these which are arrayed in white robes? and whence came they? And I said unto him, Sir, thou knowest. And he said to me, These are they which came out of great tribulation, and have washed their robes, and made them white in the blood of the Lamb. Therefore are they before the throne of God,*

*and serve Him day and night in His temple: and He that sit-
teth on the throne shall dwell among them. They shall hunger
no more, neither thirst any more; neither shall the sun light on
them, nor any heat. For the Lamb which is in the midst of the
throne shall feed them, and shall lead them unto living foun-
tains of waters: and God shall wipe away all tears from their
eyes* (Revelation 7:9-17, emphasis added).

This Scripture passage was just too beautiful to leave out a single word! I believe it reveals there will be a great number more
than just 144,000 in Heaven; don't you?

Chapter Five

Attractive Opposites

Occasionally, God uses repetition when He talks with us. Sometimes He uses it for emphasis, and sometimes for other reasons. When Peter first began ministering, he ministered only to Jews. When it came time to start ministering to Gentiles, his religion got in his way. He was a Jew, and Jews didn't believe that Gentiles could be saved. But God had other ideas. So He spoke to Peter in a vision about his error. He sent him the same fax three times (see Acts 10:9-20). He wasn't just trying to emphasize His message; He was telling Peter to conform to what He was revealing to him. On another occasion, God gave Pharaoh two dreams having the same meaning. Joseph interpreted the dreams, informing Pharaoh that the dreams were given in two forms because the matter would surely come to pass. The message of Pharaoh's dream contained good news and bad news. The good news? There's good times ahead. The bad news? They won't last! And besides that, God even revealed to Pharaoh when the market was going to crash (see Gen. 41:1-7,32-36)! God is no respecter of persons and He doesn't change. He still warns those He loves about trouble ahead. Sometimes He uses numbers in the process.

To know what God is saying, we must understand His way of using numbers. I mentioned previously that He has a unique way of revealing *opposites* in numbers. *Eleven* through *nineteen* are simply opposite of *one* through *nine*.

Eleven—Last or End

*O*NE MEANS "BEGINNING"; *eleven* means "end" or "last." In one of Jesus' parables, He hired several laborers at the eleventh hour of the day. When it came to quitting time, He told His foreman to pay them *first*, because they were hired *last* (see Mt. 20:6).

Joseph was pretty sharp when it came to interpreting dreams, but not at first:

> And [Joseph] *dreamed yet another dream, and told it his brethren, and said, Behold, I have dreamed a dream more; and, behold, the sun and the moon and the **eleven** stars made obeisance to me* (Genesis 37:9, emphasis added).

As we mentioned before, sometimes a symbol has a double meaning. If he had understood more about numbers, Joseph probably would have guessed, or at least suspected, that his brethren wouldn't bow down to him until much later in life. In fact, he represented Jesus, and Jesus' brethren still haven't bowed to Him. They won't until the eleventh hour, when they say, "Blessed is He that cometh in the name of the Lord" (Lk. 13:35b). And again, God used *eleven* twice in Deuteronomy 1:2-3 to emphasize the fact that Israel's wilderness journeys were over:

> *(There are **eleven** days' journey from Horeb by the way of mount Seir unto Kadesh-barnea.) And it came to pass in the fortieth year, in the **eleventh** month, on the first day of the month, that Moses spake unto the children of Israel....Ye have dwelt long enough in this mount....go in and possess the land...* (Deuteronomy 1:2-3,6-8, emphasis added).

Twelve—Unity or Government

*O*NE AND *ELEVEN* are easy to see. But what about *two* and *twelve*? They're also opposites. Two means "divide"; *twelve* means "join." It's really that simple. But someone is sure to balk here, and say, "No way—*twelve* means 'government'!" And it does, but only through implication. One of the primary purposes of government is to unify people. The root meaning of *twelve* is "join" or "unity," not "government." When interpreting the number *twelve*, "government" doesn't always fit. Good government produces unity, but unity doesn't always produce government.

Unity and government are closely related, but the difference between them when substituted for the number *twelve* can be readily seen in the following example. After Jesus fed the five thousand with bread and fish, His disciples, "took up of the fragments that remained twelve baskets full" (Mt. 14:20b). They gathered them up, uniting them after they were scattered—exactly what God is doing with His sheep. The purpose of church government is to unite the sheep, joining them to God through Christ. Without this understanding, the primary reason for using twelve as a symbol for government is lost.

Thirteen—Change or Rebellion

COMPARED TO *TWO* AND *TWELVE*, *three* and *thirteen* are easy! If *three* means "conformed," thirteen means to "change," and by extension, "rebel." This is confirmed at the very first mention of *thirteen* in the Bible. There were five kings joined together and for "twelve years they served Chedorlaomer, and in the thirteenth year they *rebelled*" (Gen. 14:4; see also Gen. 14:1-3; emphasis added). It doesn't get any plainer than that! I believe that's the reason America began with thirteen colonies. We started in rebellion (or was it revolution?). Anyway, I hope it doesn't end that way.

Another good Scripture demonstrating the meaning of thirteen is Jeremiah 25:3:

*From the **thirteenth** year of Josiah the son of Amon king of Judah, even unto this day, that is the three and twentieth year, the word of the Lord hath come unto me, and I have spoken unto you, rising early and speaking; but ye have not hearkened.*

If I can take the liberty to paraphrase here, Jeremiah's message says something like this: "From the time of your rebellion...even unto this day I have conformed (listened) to Him and judged you as rejected by Him, continually warning you, but you have not hearkened."

Fourteen—Double or Duplicate

BY NOW, YOU MAY BE ABLE to figure out *fourteen* through *nineteen*, but some of those numbers are rather difficult to interpret without an in-depth study. Fourteen is a good example of this difficulty; it means "double" or "duplicate." As we learned, *four* means "rule" or "reign," but it also includes the thought of the subjects who are ruled over—in other words, the whole kingdom. That makes it a little harder to identify its opposite. In fact, before we can explore the full meaning of *fourteen*, we must examine another concept concerning the teens (including *eleven*).

The Fruit of the Garden

WE'VE SAID THAT the meanings for *eleven* through *nineteen* are opposite the base numbers, but it's not always quite that simple. Sometimes there's a little more to it than that. As we mentioned before, the interpretation of some of the teens is actually the result of applying the original numbers. Or, the teen numbers can be compared to the *fruit* of a garden planted with the nine base numbers. Looking at *thirteen* and *three*, we see that rebellion and conformity are indeed opposites, but more than opposites, rebellion is the *result* of (forced) conformity.

God is the Alpha and the Omega, the beginning and the end. When He starts something, He finishes it. Therefore, if something has a beginning, it usually has an end. One produces the other. When we divide something, we often end up with two united wholes. (For example, all the people in Heaven, and all the people in hell.) When people are forced to conform, eventually they will rebel. When one man rules over another, the result is that he doubles or duplicates himself through his subject. An employer doubles his labor through an employee; a teacher replicates his knowledge in his students; a musician duplicates his skills in his protégé, etc. So a kingdom is the result of a king being duplicated in his subjects; his labor, his knowledge, his character—all are portrayed throughout his kingdom. That's the root meaning of *fourteen*, and that's the stated purpose of *the* King! King Jesus said, "Verily, verily, I say unto you, He that believeth on Me, the works that I do shall he do also; and greater works than these shall he do..." (Jn. 14:12).

Before Elijah was taken up into Heaven, he asked his servant Elisha what he could do for him as a reward for his faithfulness. Elisha seized the opportunity and asked for a double portion of Elijah's anointing. During Elijah's ministry he performed seven recorded miracles. Although Elisha had been promised a double portion, he performed only thirteen miracles during his lifetime. But God is faithful. After Elisha died and was buried, some soldiers threw a dead man into his tomb. When the dead man touched Elisha's bones, he revived and arose from the dead. Therefore Elisha was given his fourteenth miracle, completing his double portion as promised (see 2 Kings 13:21).

The following Scripture also reveals that *fourteen* is the doubling of *seven*:

> *And at that time Solomon held a feast, and all Israel with him...before the Lord our God, **seven days and seven days, even fourteen days** (1 Kings 8:65, emphasis added).*

And after satan destroyed Job's livestock, including seven thousand sheep, God restored his herd, giving him twice as much as he had before:

> *And the Lord turned the captivity of Job, when he prayed for his friends: also the Lord gave Job **twice** [double] as much as he had before....for he had **fourteen** thousand sheep... (Job 42:10,12, emphasis added).*

God commanded Moses to hold the Passover feast on the fourteenth day of the first month of the year (see Ex. 12:6). Why? Because Christ our Passover is sacrificed for us, and through Him we become like Him (see 1 Cor. 5:7). Jesus said, "Every one that is perfect shall be as his master" (Lk. 6:40b). In other words, He duplicates Himself in and through us. "Herein is our love made perfect, that we may have boldness in the day of judgment: because as He is, so are we in this world" (1 Jn. 4:17).

Fifteen—Grace or Salvation

*F*IFTEEN ISN'T QUITE SO COMPLICATED. It refers to "grace." For instance, God was gracious enough to raise Hezekiah from his deathbed and extend his life fifteen extra years after he became sick. And as an added gesture of His marvelous grace, He *saved* Jerusalem from being attacked by the king of Assyria:

> *Go, and say to Hezekiah, Thus saith the Lord, the God of David thy father, I have heard thy prayer, I have seen thy tears: behold, I will add unto thy days **fifteen** years. And I will deliver thee and this city out of the hand of the king of Assyria: and I will*

defend this city (Is. 38:5, emphasis added; see also 2 Kings 20:6).

I might add that grace is more than "unmerited favor," as it is so often defined. It's also God's divine ability reflected in man (see 1 Pet. 4:10-11).

Sixteen—Free Spirit or Likeness

S IXTEEN ISN'T QUITE as straightforward as *fifteen*. What exactly is the opposite of an image, anyway? Answer? *A free spirit, without bounds*. Isn't that what your teenage son thinks he is? (Just kidding!) The opposite of an image is whatever made the image in the first place. *Six* is like a mirror image. A mirror reverses the image it produces. God produced our flesh in His image. That means flesh is His opposite. (Boy, does that ever fit!) That's why it gives Him so much trouble! The image, our carnal self, cannot even obey Him (see Rom. 8:7). Once we understand that, we can see that the opposite of the image is the likeness of the One who produced it—God. And God is indeed a free Spirit. We might say that *six* often relates to the outward man, while *sixteen* relates more to the heart. Now that's not a steadfast rule, but it helps us better understand the relationship between the two. Another way of thinking about *sixteen* is simply *likeness*. Remember, God made us in His image *and* likeness. They're not the same thing.

Seventeen—Incomplete or Immature

T ACKLING *SEVENTEEN* IS EASY compared to the last three. It simply means "incomplete" or "immature." The opposite of the meaning of *seven* (complete) is incomplete. The normal result of becoming a mature adult is to reproduce a baby who is immature, the opposite of the parent. Probably the best scriptural example showing the meaning of *seventeen* is Joseph. He was seventeen years old when he had his first dream about his brothers bowing down to him. In his immaturity, he didn't know that he shouldn't tell them! He learned pretty quick though; his brothers were good teachers (see Gen. 37:2-5). He was thirty-nine years old before his dreams came to pass. He was considerably more mature by then. And no, his age isn't listed in the Bible, but one can accurately compute it by the information given. You can also almost guess it by simply understanding the meaning of numbers!

Eighteen—Put On or Overcome

*E*IGHTEEN IS ANOTHER EASY ONE. It means "put on." Jesus used it in this way on two different occasions during His ministry. The first time referred to God's judgment falling upon some sinful men:

> *Or those* **eighteen**, *upon whom the tower in Siloam fell, and slew them, think ye that they were sinners above all men that dwelt in Jerusalem?* (Luke 13:4)

The second was concerning a woman whom satan had bound:

> *And, behold, there was a woman which had a spirit of infirmity* **eighteen** *years, and was bowed together, and could in no wise lift up herself.* [After delivering and healing her, Jesus said,]...*ought not this woman, being a daughter of Abraham, whom satan hath bound, lo, these* **eighteen** *years, be loosed from this bond on the sabbath day?* (Luke 13:11,16)

Nineteen—Lack or Ashamed

*N*INETEEN IS ALSO SIMPLE, but needs a little more explanation. Because *nine* means "fruit" or "harvest," *nineteen* simply means "no fruit" or "no harvest." When there is a *lack* of fruitfulness, we call the land *barren*. In the Old Testament, when a woman was barren, she was ashamed. So by implication, *nineteen* can also mean "ashamed." Joab's army had defeated the army of Abner, but when the battle was over and Joab was able to gather his people together, he discovered that he had lost nineteen men and Asahel:

> *And Joab returned from following Abner: and when he had gathered all the people together, there* **lacked** *of David's servants* **nineteen** *men and Asahel* (2 Samuel 2:30, emphasis added).

Joab may not have been ashamed, but he certainly couldn't have been proud of his accomplishments; he lost his brother Asahel in the battle.

In review, every symbol has a root meaning. Because we're talking about numbers, we can say that each symbol should be reduced to its common denominator—the root. Each root grows branches, and sometimes, even branches grow branches. But once we determine the root, we can easily follow the chain of deduction that leads to each branch, as you can see in the following summary, which includes the primary implied meaning along with each root: *Eleven* is "last" or "end"; *twelve* is "unity" or "government"; *thirteen* is "change" or "rebellion"; *fourteen* is "double" or "duplicate"; *fifteen* is "grace" or "salvation"; *sixteen* is "free spirit" or "likeness"; *seventeen* is "incomplete" or "immature"; *eighteen* is "put on" or "overcome"; and *nineteen* is "lack" or "ashamed." As you see, each extended branch is closely related to its root or source.

Chapter Six

Simple Solutions

Eleven Hundred

THE MEANINGS OF OTHER ROUND NUMBERS in the hundreds and thousands follow the same line of reasoning that we've uncovered in the preceding five chapters. If *eleven* is last, then *eleven hundred* has to be the last of the last. In fact, *eleven hundred* appears only three times in Scripture, and all three times it refers to the root of all evil—silver. (The Greek phrase translated "love of money" in Paul's famous saying, "The *love of money* is the root of all evil" is literally, "fondness for silver" [see 1 Tim. 6:10, emphasis added].) Delilah betrayed Samson for eleven hundred pieces of silver (see Judg. 16:5). I'm sure her disloyalty earned her a place on the tail end of his list of favorites.

The other two references to eleven hundred pieces of silver are also found in Judges. The silver is rather tarnished here, too. It became a curse unto Israel because they used it to make a molten image:

> *And [Micah] said to his mother, "The **eleven hundred** shekels of silver that were taken from you, and on which you put a curse, even saying it in my ears—here is the silver with me; I took it."...So when he had returned the **eleven hundred** shekels of silver to his mother, his mother said, "I had wholly dedicated the silver from my hand to the Lord for my son, to make a carved*

image and a molded image; now therefore, I will return it to you (Judges 17:2-3 NKJ).

After they cursed the silver and made an idol out of it, it's obvious that God put it last on His list, too. He doesn't seem to like idols very much.

Twelve Hundred

*T*WELVE HUNDRED IS QUITE UNIQUE. Although twelve is mentioned 132 times in the Bible, *twelve hundred* occurs only once:

And it came to pass, that in the fifth year of king Rehoboam Shishak king of Egypt came up against Jerusalem, because they had transgressed against the Lord, with **twelve hundred** *chariots, and threescore thousand horsemen: and the people were without number that came with him out of Egypt; the Lubims, the Sukkiims, and the Ethiopians* (2 Chronicles 12:2-3, emphasis added).

Twelve means "unity," and this multitude was certainly unified against Jerusalem. By the way, this Scripture is also a good example where the root meaning works well (unity), but the branch meaning (government) just won't fit. There are a couple other numbers in this Scripture that are worth noticing—*five* and *sixty thousand*. This was a big operation against Jerusalem. God turned the bad and the ugly loose on them, and left out the good altogether.

It looks like we've just run out of numbers. *Eleven hundred* is used three times; *twelve hundred* once; and *thirteen hundred* through *nineteen hundred* are not even in the Book. But if we stay on track we can figure out what they all mean.

Thirteen Hundred

*T*HIRTEEN MEANS "REBELLION," and *hundred* is "fullness," so *thirteen hundred* simply means fullness of rebellion. This number brings to mind a revelation that God gave me many years ago. God is reluctant to destroy a person or nation until they have fully rebelled against Him. Once they do, they reach a point of no return, and He has no other recourse but to destroy them. That's the reason He commanded Israel to kill everyone in Canaan. Their cup of iniquity was so full, there was no room for redemption.

God actually waited four hundred years before sending Israel into the land. He told Abraham that his grandchildren would have to wait in Egypt for awhile; "But in the fourth generation they shall come hither again: for the iniquity of the Amorites is not yet full" (Gen. 15:16).

Fourteen Hundred Through Nineteen Hundred

*F*OURTEEN HUNDRED COVERS the whole kingdom; *fifteen hundred* means fullness of grace, or radically saved; *sixteen hundred* is free as a bird; *seventeen hundred* says he's just a baby; *eighteen hundred* is pressed down and running over (or bankruptcy, whichever comes first); and *nineteen hundred* is totally lacking in whatever counts. Now, what about the *thousands*? Let's take a look.

Eleven Thousand

*I*N THE SAME WAY that we were able to figure out the *hundreds*, we can discover the meaning of the *thousands*. Although *eleven thousand* is not in the Bible, *eleven* means "last" and *thousands* speak of "maturity" (completeness). The concept of largeness that we previously discovered is also retained in these numbers. Using this definition, *eleven thousand* should mean something like the end of time. Maybe that is why God hasn't used it. We're not there yet.

Twelve Thousand

*T*WELVE THOUSAND IS USED thirteen times in Scripture and the very first Scripture reveals its meaning, "So there were delivered out of the thousands of Israel, a thousand of every tribe, twelve thousand armed for war" (Num. 31:5). Beautiful unity, complete unity, every tribe perfectly represented and joined together for a common cause.

Another Scripture showing complete unity is this one: "And so it was, that all that fell that day, both of men and women, were twelve thousand, even all the men of Ai" (Josh. 8:25). It's obvious that they all died together, every one of them.

Thirteen Thousand

*T*HIRTEEN THOUSAND IS NOT in the Bible either, but that's understandable; God already killed all of them because they fully rebelled back in *thirteen hundred*. (Just kidding!) *Thirteen thousand* simply means complete rebellion. Although the number isn't mentioned, one Scripture that shows how God feels about rebellion is Deuteronomy 21:18-21:

> *If a man have a stubborn and rebellious son, which will not obey the voice of his father, or the voice of his mother, and that, when they have chastened him, will not hearken unto them: Then shall his father and his mother lay hold on him, and bring him out unto the elders of his city, and unto the gate of his place; and they shall say unto the elders of his city, This our son is stubborn and rebellious, he will not obey our voice; he is a glutton, and a drunkard. And all the men of his city shall stone him with stones, that he die: so shalt thou put evil away from among you; and all Israel shall hear, and fear.*

Fourteen Thousand

AS FOR *FOURTEEN THOUSAND*, the Scripture that captures the meaning best of all is Job 42:12:

> *So the Lord blessed the latter end of Job more than his beginning: for he had **fourteen thousand** sheep, and six thousand camels, and a thousand yoke of oxen, and a thousand she asses.*

Fourteen means "double," and in this Scripture, God is doubling back to Job everything he had lost (which was *everything*!) during the horrible trial he endured. Job received full compensation.

Before going on to another Scripture that further illustrates God's use of *fourteen thousand*, let's examine a little background information about His penalty for sin. First look at Isaiah 40:2:

> *Speak ye comfortably to Jerusalem, and cry unto her, that her warfare is accomplished, that her iniquity is pardoned: **for she hath received of the Lord's hand double for all her sins*** (emphasis added).

Also notice Jeremiah 16:18: "And first I will recompense their iniquity and their sin double; because they have defiled my land...." And finally, Jeremiah 17:18: "Let them be confounded that persecute me...and destroy them with double destruction." Notice that in each case, just as God reimbursed Job double for his *righteousness*, these people were recompensed double for their *iniquity*. Now, with that thought in mind, let's look at another Scripture:

> *But on the morrow all the congregation of the children of Israel murmured against Moses and against Aaron, saying, Ye have killed the people of the Lord....And Moses said unto Aaron...go quickly unto the congregation, and make an atonement for them: for there is wrath gone out from the Lord; the plague is begun....Now they that died in the plague were* **fourteen thousand and seven hundred**, *beside them that died about the matter of Korah* (Numbers 16:41,46,49, emphasis added).

They troubled Moses and Aaron, so God visited them with double trouble, or as Jeremiah said, "double destruction." Of course, *seven hundred* means that God's judgment was a full and complete "recompense of reward" for their sin (see 2 Thess. 1:6; Heb. 2:2-3).

Fifteen Thousand

*F*IFTEEN THOUSAND IS USED only once in the Bible, and it refers to the last stronghold that Gideon defeated when by the grace of God he delivered Israel in the days of the judges. In this passage it signifies complete salvation:

> *Now Zebah and Zalmunna were in Karkor, and their hosts with them, about* **fifteen thousand men, all that were left of all the hosts of the children of the east:** *for there fell an hundred and twenty thousand men that drew sword* (Judges 8:10, emphasis added).

Sixteen Thousand

T HE WAY GOD USES *sixteen thousand* in Numbers is ingenious:

> *And all the gold of the offering that they offered up to the Lord, of the captains of thousands...was sixteen thousand seven hundred and fifty shekels. (For the men of war had taken spoil,* **every man for himself.***)* (Numbers 31:52-53 emphasis added).

Sixteen means "free spirit," and of course, *thousand* means "complete," so completely free is the picture, or as God puts it, "every man for himself." Now, is that neat, or what?

Seventeen Thousand

*S*EVENTEEN THOUSAND IS A CONTRADICTION of terms. *Seventeen* means "incomplete" or "immature," and *thousand* means "mature." Figure that one out! This number is used only once in the Bible, and there it emphasizes the *thousands* viewpoint and ignores *seventeen*. Curious? Look it up (see 1 Chron. 7:11).

Eighteen Thousand

*E*IGHTEEN THOUSAND is no problem. In Second Samuel 8:13, David fought against the Syrians and as we say in the South, "He evermore put one on them!" "And David gat him a name when he returned from smiting of the Syrians in the valley of salt, being eighteen thousand men." This number is also used during one of Israel's many civil wars:

> *And Benjamin went forth against them...the second day, and destroyed down to the ground of the children of Israel again eighteen thousand men; all these drew the sword* (Judges 20:25).

Although the tribe of Benjamin eventually lost, before going down, the little tribe got in one last hit on Israel. The full implication of this civil strife isn't clear until you get to Judges 21:3, "And said, O Lord God of Israel, why is this come to pass in Israel, that there should be today one tribe lacking in Israel?" As a result of their fighting amongst themselves, Benjamin came within a hair's breath of being completely destroyed.

Nineteen Thousand

*A*ND NOW WE COME to the end. Last, but not least, that is. Although it's not mentioned in the Bible, *nineteen thousand* means totally ashamed; fully useless; completely drained; utterly barren; etc.

A Simple System

*I*N SUMMARY, *eleven hundred* and *eleven thousand* are similar, as are *twelve hundred* and *twelve thousand*, all the way through *nineteen hundred* and *nineteen thousand*. There are minor differences, but they're mostly in quantity, not quality. As one can see, there are really only nine numbers to learn. Then, by learning to measure these base numbers by tens, hundreds, and thousands, one can achieve full understanding of the system. For the opposites, or results, one need only reverse the root meanings. And so, one can master the entire numerical system in short order. Simple, isn't it?

Chapter Seven

Coloring Within the Lines

MANY DREAMS ARE IN TECHNICOLOR, but not all. Most dreamers are unaware that part of what they dream is in grayscale; they only notice certain things that are colored. Splashes of color give added meaning to our dreams and are every bit as significant as numbers. But searching out their meanings poses a slight problem. We learned the meaning of numbers directly from the Bible, but colors are a little different. Several important colors cannot be found in the Bible. The Bible is not exactly printed in grayscale, but it doesn't have pastels, either. In fact, it's a lot like our dreams; it only uses colors when they're needed to supply specific information. That gives us a clue. We can use the Bible to learn how God uses colors, and then use the same reasoning to stay within the lines when interpreting colors of our own.

In Chapter One, we discussed the four ways that symbols obtain meaning: inherent characteristics; personal experience; culture; and Scripture. When we studied numbers, we used Scripture as the sole basis for our definitions. These definitions came directly from creation and God's dealings with man. But in passing, we noted that culture also influences the meaning of certain symbols used in the Bible. So does inherent character. In fact, the primary characteristic of many symbols is a direct product of creation. A wolf devours lambs naturally, and lambs are defenseless by nature. Because inherent character is also used to determine the meaning of symbols in Scripture, we should consider it when searching for the meaning of colors, whether within or without Scripture.

Since there is no linear order to colors, when possible we will discuss them in the order suggested by the inherent characteristics given to them in creation. In the beginning, God started with darkness and then made light. We'll begin the same way. Darkness is the absence of light; black is the absence of color. So we'll ride in on a black horse right out of the pages of the Bible.

Black Is Lack

THERE'S PROBABLY FEW PASSAGES of Scripture more controversial than the four horses of the apocalypse. One of those horses is black:

And when He had opened the third seal, I heard the third beast say, Come and see. And I beheld, and lo a black horse; and he that sat on him had a pair of balances in his hand. And I heard a voice in the midst of the four beasts say, A measure of wheat for a penny, and three measures of barley for a penny; and see thou hurt not the oil and the wine (Revelation 6:5-6).

Although we want to avoid the aforementioned controversy, you should know that this passage refers directly to the terrible famine prophesied by Amos that occurred during the Dark Ages:

Behold, the days come, saith the Lord God, that I will send a famine in the land, not a famine of bread, nor a thirst for water, but of hearing the words of the Lord (Amos 8:11).

The balances the rider was holding measured food, and not much at that. It was famine portions. A penny was a full day's wages, and a measure of wheat only one meal. During that spiritual famine, men worked all day for just one meal.

Because darkness is the absence of light, when light appears, darkness disappears. So the primary meaning of *black* is "lack." Ignorance is the lack of knowledge, so *black* may indicate ignorance. In our culture, it's also the color used to recognize death. We wear it to funerals to signify our grief over losing a loved one. Death is the absence of life, subsequently death is an extended meaning of *black*.

Black often means bad news, such as the report that Job received when satan destroyed his flocks and children (see Job 1:13-18). Job also used *black* to describe his condition when he was physically afflicted, "My skin is black upon me, and my bones are burned with heat" (Job 30:30

Another way to envision the meaning of *black* is to think of the black darkness of night and what happens during that time, as we see in Proverbs 7:9-10:

In the twilight, in the evening, in the black and dark night. And, behold, there met him a woman with the attire of an harlot, and subtle of heart.

So *black* can mean wickedness, evil, and sin. Famine; grief; death; ignorance; wickedness; evil; sin—they're all ugly! However, almost all symbols have both positive and negative meanings. Therefore, black can also mean beautiful, "I am *black*, but comely, O ye daughters of Jerusalem..." (Song 1:5). If that wasn't true, Ford and Chevrolet wouldn't make so many black cars.

In addition, the opposite of lack is substance, so *black* can also indicate substance! In fact, it can mean the very opposite of drought and famine—abundance! An example? Read what happened when Elijah prayed for rain:

And it came to pass [as Elijah prayed] *at the seventh time, that* [his servant] *said, Behold, there ariseth a little cloud out of the sea, like a man's hand. And he said, Go up, say unto Ahab, Prepare thy chariot, and get thee down, that the rain stop thee not. And it came to pass...that the heaven was* **black** *with clouds and wind,* **and there was a great rain**...(1 Kings 18:44-45, emphasis added).

Blue Is Spiritual

NEXT COMES *BLUE*. It's very similar to *black* and also has a double meaning. First, *blue* is the color of the sky on a beautiful day, so it means "heavenly." In the beginning God created the [blue] heavens and the earth (Gen. 1:1 NKJ). Aaron wore a beautiful blue robe every time he went into God's presence, signifying that he was entering into the heavenly realms. "And thou shalt make the [priest's] robe of the ephod all of blue" (Ex. 28:31).

Aaron's robe was part of "the patterns of things in the heavens..." (Heb. 9:23b).

The blue sky is composed of air, which symbolizes spirit, so *blue* can mean "spirit" or "spiritual." In fact, that is one of the most common usages that I've encountered. It also appears to be the root meaning, although these two, *heavenly* and *spiritual*, are often interchangeable, because that which is heavenly is spiritual. (Some spiritual things aren't heavenly, so the reverse isn't always true.) Jesus said that His words were spirit; therefore, another branch for *blue* is God's Word (see Jn. 6:63). For example, a blue washcloth may refer to, "the washing of water by the word" (Eph. 5:26b), or spiritual cleansing.

And mentioning water, another part of God's marvelous creation is the deep blue sea. Anyone who has ever seen satellite pictures of the earth is struck by its beauty. The lofty, swirling clouds and the seas' awesome blue color are spellbinding. In certain passages of Scripture the sea represents either God or man, depending on the context, and the sea's color reinforces this symbolism. Isaiah declared, "The earth shall be full of the knowledge of the Lord, as the waters cover the sea" (Is. 11:9b). But he also compared it to wicked and sinful men, "But the wicked are like the troubled sea, when it cannot rest, whose waters cast up mire and dirt" (Is. 57:20).

Then he used it as a symbol for the Gentile nations, "...the abundance of the sea shall be converted unto thee, the forces of the Gentiles shall come unto thee" (Is. 60:5).

Returning to the subject of the sky, God's Spirit is *always* heavenly; man's spirit is not. Neither are men always happy. When they're sad, we say they are "singing the blues." So instead of heavenly, *blue* may indicate that someone is down in the dumps. A very light shade of *blue* sometimes indicates the spirit of man, while any shade of *blue* can symbolize God's Spirit. In another instance, after a friend of mine died, I once dreamed that I saw a picture of her. Her dress was an incredibly beautiful color of deep blue. As I watched, I saw her picture ascend out of sight. I awoke knowing that she was with God, eternal in the Heavens.

In that dream, *blue* represented salvation. It can also mean healing. "The blueness of a wound cleanseth away evil..." (Prov.

20:30). But when one considers that *blue* often symbolizes God's Spirit and sometimes His Word, that's not too surprising. After all, "He sent His word, and healed them," didn't He? (Ps. 107:20a).

When painted objects are used as symbols, the paint's condition is also symbolic. Whether the paint is glossy or dull, off-color or the wrong color (pale horse, blue elephant, etc.), all mean one thing or another. So a light blue house with paint that is chipped and peeled may represent someone wounded or offended. It's not uncommon for a house to represent its owner, and in this instance the decaying paint job may denote the need for spiritual repairs. Because *blue* is considered a "cool" color, it could even be saying that the person who lives there has grown cool toward others. This principle of paint condition, dark and light shades, and right or wrong color applies throughout the spectrum. A whole rainbow of colors exists with many different shades of meaning.

A Bow in the Cloud

SPEAKING OF RAINBOWS, the rainbow itself has a beautiful meaning. It denotes a covenant, an everlasting covenant:

> *I do set My bow in the cloud, and it shall be for a token of a covenant between Me and the earth....And the bow shall be in the cloud; and I will look upon it, that I may remember the everlasting covenant between God and every living creature of all flesh that is upon the earth* (Genesis 9:13,16; see also Hebrews 13:20).

The full spectrum of God's love and wisdom is seen through the knowledge He gave Paul. Paul fans out love's many dimensions the way a prism spreads light's brilliant colors (see 1 Cor. 13). Also, he mentions the spectrum of God's wisdom in Ephesians:

> *His intent was that now, through the church, the manifold wisdom of God should be made known to the rulers and authorities in the heavenly realms* (Ephesians 3:10 NIV).

The Greek word translated *manifold* means "variegated," like the many colors of the rainbow. We'll take a peek through Paul's prism as we continue our colorful examination.

More Shades of Blue

GETTING BACK TO *BLUE*, since *blue* can represent God's Spirit, by extension it can also represent His love because God *is* love. And the fact that He's the God of peace, *blue* can symbolize peaceful. Similarly, God is light, and as we've already discussed, *blue* symbolizes His Word because His Word is light. Then, there's always the traditional meaning—baby boys dressed in blue. With so many possible definitions to choose from, it's not hard to see that one should pay very close attention to the context in which *blue* is used before trying to decide exactly what it conveys.

Color Combinations

ONE MORE THOUGHT before we move on. Sometimes we dream of a combination of colors—*black and blue*, for instance. If someone takes a pounding, we may say, "He was beat black and blue." It's a good way to describe a severe beating, and it can certainly mean that in a dream, too. *Black* signifies pain and suffering, and *blue* a sorrowful spirit. As we continue, we'll see more combinations, and find that *black* is more often than not the second color.

Green Equals Life

ALTHOUGH, AT THIS POINT, we could go in several different directions, we will follow the order of creation. After God made the heavens and the earth, spoke light into existence, and divided the waters, He covered the earth with greenery. "And God said, Let the earth bring forth grass, the herb yielding seed, and the fruit tree yielding fruit after his kind, whose seed is in itself, upon the earth: and it was so" (Gen. 1:11).

The first plant mentioned here is grass. The world is covered with grass on every continent and every nation. Live grass is green, and the root meaning for *green* is "life." One can tell whether grass is alive or not by simply noticing if it is green. When it turns brown, it's dead.

Trees and most other plants are also green. Some plants stay green throughout the seasons; others lose their leaves in fall and wait for spring before being resurrected into new life. Herein lies a clue—*green* can denote resurrected life. Likewise, an evergreen tree may mean eternal life, because it never dies and stays green continuously, or at least it appears to be everlasting.

In a negative sense, *green* can refer to the temporal state of man's flesh. Peter said, *"For all flesh is as grass,* and all the glory of man as the flower of grass. The grass withereth, and the flower thereof falleth away" (1 Pet. 1:24, emphasis added).

Jesus also used *green* to signify His flesh. When they were leading Him to Golgotha to crucify Him, He said, "For if they do these things in a green tree, what shall be done in the dry?" (Lk. 23:31)

So *green* and *grass* have much in common. The inherent characteristics of grass determine the symbolic meanings of both *grass* and *green*. The green color of grass indicates that it is alive. It multiplied and covered the whole earth, even as Adam was commanded to do. And when some grasses and other similar evergreen plants defy the seasons and refuse to die, they imitate eternity and give us a unique symbol for everlasting life.

Brown and Tan

As WE MENTIONED, when grass dies, it turns brown. In the same way that green grass indicates life in its different forms, its color in death reveals the root meaning for *brown*. In essence, *brown* is the opposite of *green—death* instead of life. When we live in the flesh, we are *green*. When we repent and die to sin, we turn *brown*. A repentant person is humble. Therefore, *brown* often denotes humility or one who is lowly. By extension, *brown* can also mean common, ordinary, or poor, like a person carrying a sack lunch in a brown paper bag. *Tan* is simply a lighter shade of brown, and denotes a similar meaning. In fact, *tan* is the color of desert sand and has the connotation of barrenness. Repentance is sometimes indicated by tan clothing or shoes.

Christmas Colors

THERE IS ANOTHER COLOR closely associated with green—*red*. At first glance there seems to be no connection between the two, other than they are used together as decorations at Christmas time. However, the connection comes from the fact that *red* is conceived as a "warm" color, and *green* often refers to "flesh."

Red denotes "passion." A passionate suitor buys red roses for his beloved. A matador waves a red cape before a charging bull. An angry person is said to be "seeing red." All these portray the concept of passion, and passion is one of the characteristics of flesh. Therein lies the connection. *Green* corresponds to flesh, subsequently *red* and *green* can indicate passionate flesh. Ever watch a kid on Christmas morning?

Another common use for red is on stop signs and red lights. Interestingly enough, *green* signifies "go," while *red* means "stop." By extension, *red* can mean danger, as in the bull charging the matador's cape above. And if the bull connects, the matador's blood may run red, giving us one more metaphor for *red*—blood. Blood can mean so many things that we'll not even discuss the subject in this book, except to give its basic, root meaning—*life*. So red's danger signal can even include loss of life. In fact, the red horse of Revelation 6:4 portrayed just that—persecution and martyrdom:

> *And there went out another horse that was red: and power was given to him that sat thereon to take peace from the earth, and that they should kill one another: and there was given unto him a great sword.*

Danger Signals

AND SPEAKING OF DANGER, watch out for *orange*! Danger may not be the primary meaning, but I've discovered that in many dreams, danger is a very common interpretation for *orange*. In fact, one of nature's primary warning colors is bright orange. South America has brilliant orange frogs that are so poisonous the natives use them as a source of poison for their hunting darts. Orange and black monarch butterflies are poisonous. And who wouldn't run from a tiger? Of course, not all orange creatures are dangerous. But every symbol has its opposite, doesn't it?

The root meaning for *orange* is "energy" or "power." Power is inherent in many orange things that God created. The earth's primary source of energy, the sun, was made on the fourth day and is rather orange in color. Closer at hand, fire is a chief source of power and it's usually orange. It can be dangerous, too. Fire is often associated with spiritual power. In Acts 1:8, Jesus told His disciples that they would receive power after the Holy Ghost came upon them, and in Acts 2:3-4, they did. Flames of fire were seen resting upon them when that happened. Those flames were probably orange.

One dream that particularly interested me was a dream where a woman and her family were attacked by fierce dragons. She discovered that her only effective defense was oranges! Even pieces of the oranges were sufficient to ward them off. The interpretation? If Golden Delicious apples can stand for wise counsel, as in Proverbs 25:11, "A word fitly spoken is like apples of gold in pictures of silver," then couldn't a bag of oranges represent God's powerful promises such as Psalm 91:13? "Thou shalt tread upon the lion and adder: the young lion and the dragon shalt thou trample under feet."

A Dangerous Combination

You MAY HAVE NOTICED the color combination of the Monarch butterflies and tigers mentioned previously. Orange often spells trouble, but when combined with black, it's just plain bad news! Pay attention. It's nearly always a warning! On the other hand, it can spell bad news for the devil, too. The Holy Ghost baptism has really given him a hard time. I once dreamed about one of the old-time, Holy Ghost-filled preachers where God compared him to a tiger in my dream. The orange and black stripes were plain to see. In another dream, I bought an antique sports car. I paid $350 for it. I was going to have it painted. I could see the colors in my mind's eye—bright fire orange with a black top! The paint job was expected to cost me $700. I'm not sure that I've finished paying for it yet.

A Clear-cut Combination

Now THAT WE'VE RETURNED to the subject of black-color combinations, there is no doubt *black and white* is the most common combination of all. And there's a very common meaning for it—right and wrong. Have you ever heard someone say something like, "He won't compromise. With him, everything's either black or white"? *Legalistic* is another word for it, or *opinionated*. Of course, to that person, it's clear-cut; there are simply no gray areas.

But we'll get to *gray* in a second. On the positive side, *black and white* can be saying, "Hey, can't you see? It's plain as day!"

Sometimes "salt and pepper" depicts integration—mixing it up. At other times, as when we speak of a black and white movie, we are simply referring to lack of color. And whether we're awake or dreaming, the word *color* can mean "flavor." So the lack of color can mean mundane, dull, uninviting, boring, etc., but dreams usually depict this with gray instead of black and white.

A "Gray" Area

GRAY CAN MEAN CONFUSION, like being in a gray fog, or *without clear guide lines or boundaries*. It's not unusual to hear someone say, "That's a gray area; I'm just not sure what to do there." Smoke is gray, too, and "Where there's smoke, there's fire." So gray smoke can warn you of trouble brewing, or worse, let you know what just happened:

> And [Abraham] *looked toward Sodom and Gomorrah, and toward all the land of the plain, and beheld, and, lo, the smoke of the country went up as the smoke of a furnace* (Genesis 19:28).

Just how gray is *gray?* The shade of gray depends on the amount of black and the amount of white mixed together. The more black, the darker the gray, and vice versa. So noticing whether something is simply a little off-white, or a darker shade of gray, can be informative when interpreting your dreams.

Pure White

As WE'VE ALREADY DISCUSSED, the opposite of gray is clear-cut, distinct, without doubt or hesitation; it's either black or white. If it's white, it's *pure*, and righteous altogether—or pure evil! In the Old Testament, God taught Moses how to determine if leprosy was cured or not:

> And the priest shall look on the plague in the skin of the flesh: and when the hair in the plague is turned **white**, and the plague in sight be deeper than the skin of his flesh, it is a plague of leprosy: and the priest shall look on him, and pronounce him **unclean** (Leviticus 13:3, emphasis added).

Some people have a way of "getting under your skin." When you're offended by them, you suffer from spiritual leprosy. It's contagious! And strange enough, contrary to many Christians' belief that *white* means right (righteousness, that is), in this Scripture, *white* portrays a plague and its uncleanness. But even Christians sometimes tell "little white lies," so they shouldn't be surprised that *white* has its opposite, too.

In fact, that brings up another use for *white* that I've encountered in dreams a little too often—self-righteousness. Like a pregnant bride in a white wedding gown, we usually try to hide the truth about ourselves, sometimes even from our own self. God reveals it to us in private dreams so that He won't have to humble us publicly.

White is mentioned in Genesis four times, and it's used negatively one out of the four: "When the chief baker saw that the interpretation [of another man's dream] was good, he said unto Joseph, I also was in my dream, and, behold, I had three *white* baskets on my head" (Gen. 40:16, emphasis added). But his white baskets meant bad news. Joseph correctly interpreted them to mean three days before the baker would be hanged by Pharaoh.

The Bible doesn't mention *white* in the record of creation, but there certainly were a large number of white birds created on the fifth day. The Holy Spirit is usually depicted as a white dove. On the other hand, a white goose can mean pure stupidity; as the saying goes, "He's like a goose; he wakes up in a new world every day." And yet still, a white swan needs no explanation. Its natural beauty and gracefulness says it all.

None More Precious Than Gold

THE ONLY COLOR ACTUALLY FOUND in the record of the original creation is gold. The river that watered the Garden of Eden had four branches: "The name of the first is Pison [increase, Heb.]...where there is gold; and the gold of that land is good..." (Gen. 2:11-12).

When the Bible says, "the gold of that land is good," it implies there's gold of other lands that's not so good. *Gold* means "glory." From the beginning, God shows us that all "glory" is not good. Or as Jeremiah puts it, "Thus saith the Lord, Let not the wise man glory in his wisdom, neither let the mighty man glory in his might, let not the rich man glory in his riches" (Jer. 9:23). Why? Because God has decreed, "That no flesh should glory in His presence....[instead] He that glorieth, let him glory in the Lord" (1 Cor. 1:29,31). You see, the gold of God's original creation is not only good, it's God's! "The silver is Mine, and the gold is Mine, saith the Lord of hosts" (Hag. 2:8).

God doesn't really care for the natural gold; He doesn't need it. He made it for man. Just don't take His! It may be hazardous to your health:

> *And upon a set day Herod, arrayed in royal apparel, sat upon his throne, and made an oration unto them. And the people gave a shout, saying, It is the voice of a god, and not of a man. And immediately the angel of the Lord smote him, because he gave not God the glory: and he was eaten of worms, and gave up the ghost* (Acts 12:21-23).

Self-glorification is a snare, both for the fool who glorifies himself, and for those who foolishly honor the fool. "For if there should come into your assembly a man with gold rings....and you pay attention..." (Jas. 2:2-3 NKJ). Instead, we're supposed to, "Mind not high things, but condescend to men of low estate. Be not wise in your own conceits" (Rom. 12:16b), but "...be clothed with humility..." (1 Pet. 5:5).

Although the root meaning for *gold* is "glory," it has a lot of other meanings, too. One is "wealth," because of gold's great value, and by extension, "prosperity." When Moses brought Israel out of Egypt, they hadn't gone far before God called Moses up on the mountaintop to give him the ten commandments. While Moses was gone, Aaron took the Israelites' gold earrings and formed them into a golden calf to worship (see Ex. 32:2-8). He used their *earrings* to signify that he was telling them what they wanted to hear. We have some Aarons in our day too. He also used *gold* earrings because *gold* meant wealth. He made them a golden *calf* because cattle signified prosperity. Cattle was their livelihood. When the herds increased, they had a "bull market." When bears ate the cattle, they lost their wealth, and the first "bear market" was born. Things haven't changed much in church *or* in the market, have they?

Another meaning for *gold* is "rare," because God didn't create much of it. That's why it's so valuable. And one of the simplest and most often used extensions is "wisdom." We sometimes act like He didn't create much of that, either. In fact, when people are "Professing themselves to be wise, they bec[o]me fools" (Rom. 1:22). Actually, most rich people glory in their wisdom more than in their money. We've come to think that the two go together. It's not too unusual to hear the sarcastic remark, "If you're so smart, why aren't you rich?" So if I'm rich, I must be smart, right? On the other hand, dreaming of finding gold coins may mean that you really are getting smarter. God may use the symbol of *gold* to confirm that He's giving someone the spirit of wisdom and revelation.

There are several more symbolic meanings for *gold*. Even silence can be golden. But at the right time, so can words: "A word fitly spoken is like apples of gold in pictures of silver" (Prov. 25:11). Another common meaning for *gold* is "unchanging." Gold doesn't tarnish. It's one of the few things in nature that doesn't change. That is one of the reasons gold makes good idols. It even qualifies as a stand-in for God. He never changes. However, neither does the devil. He's always greedy. He's always trying to steal God's glory and make it his own, because his own glory is *fools' gold.*

Gold is one of two things that either gets its name from its color, or gives its color its name; I'm not sure which. In dreams, gold is gold regardless of whether you're talking about the color or the metal. If you dream something is gold in color, or something is made of gold, basically, it means the same thing. On the other hand, if something is gold-plated, it may not be as valuable as it first appears. If it's solid gold, it's as valuable as it can get—24 carat—genuine. Glory, wealth, and prosperity; treasures of wisdom and knowledge; wise counsel and unchanging riches; beauty and value; all are embodied in gold.

The Search for Silver

SILVER IS THE OTHER UNIQUE COLOR/METAL that gets its name from its color or gives its color its name. *Silver* means "knowledge." There are few things clearer in Scripture than the definition of *silver:*

*Yea, if thou criest after **knowledge**, and liftest up thy voice for understanding; if thou seekest her as **silver**, and searchest for her as for hid treasures; then shalt thou understand the fear of the Lord, **and find the knowledge of God** (Proverbs 2:3-4, emphasis added).*

From this Scripture one can readily see that dreaming of finding silver coins, cups, bowls, etc., can represent receiving knowledge. With this thought in mind, the passage, "A word fitly spoken is like apples of gold in pictures of silver" (Prov. 25:11) becomes even more significant.

Silver and Gold

THE SILVER BACKGROUND for the golden apples represents adequate knowledge of the situation being addressed. Wisdom plus knowledge equals understanding. Both Proverbs and Paul placed these three sisters together:

That their hearts might be...knit together...unto all riches of the full assurance of understanding...of the mystery of God, and of the Father, and of Christ; in whom are hid all the treasures of wisdom and knowledge (Colossians 2:2-3).

Notice Paul's use of the metaphors, *"riches...of understanding"* and *"treasures of wisdom and knowledge."* One's treasure makes one rich. Likewise, wisdom and knowledge combined gives us, "full assurance of understanding," which is faith! Now isn't that interesting?

Like *gold*, *silver* color and *silver* metal mean about the same thing. Unlike *gold*, *silver* tarnishes. This gives an added dimension to *silver* as a symbol. Some things need constant polishing, especially relationships! Combinations of *gold* and *silver* may be used to portray wisdom and knowledge as a team. Gold and silver tapestry and clothes are not uncommon in dreams. But clothes don't always mean what you might think. Sometimes people clothe themselves with spirits. Paul admonished the Roman church, "But put ye on the Lord Jesus Christ" (Rom. 13:14a). One can wear the devil, too, "As he clothed himself with cursing like as with his garment, so let it come into his bowels like water..." (Ps. 109:18). And as we mentioned before, we're supposed to be clothed with humility.

In fables, and sometimes in dreams, the spirit of death comes wearing a black, hooded cloak. In contrast to this, dreaming of someone wearing a beautiful gold and silver suit or robe may indicate that he or she is clothed with wisdom and knowledge.

Royal Purple

OYAL ROBES ARE USUALLY PURPLE, embroidered in gold. The reason? The *purple* stands for the king's *royalty* and the *gold* trim his *glory*. *Purple* also implies virtue, "He that ruleth over men must be just, ruling in the fear of God" (2 Sam. 23:3b). Well, that's the idea, but beware, Jezebel can wear purple, too.

Like virtue, in Bible days purple dye was valuable because it was comparatively rare. Paul encountered a virtuous woman on his second missionary journey:

And a certain woman named Lydia, a seller of purple, of the city of Thyatira, which worshiped God, heard us: whose heart the Lord opened, that she attended unto the things which were spoken of Paul (Acts 16:14).

Blushing Brides and Hot Pink Shorts

INK IS ANOTHER COLOR closely associated with clothing. Little baby girls dressed in pink are the epitome of sweetness and innocence. Another distinct meaning is chaste, or modest. And who hasn't heard of a blushing bride? In another sense, *pink* may indicate that God has fulfilled one of His promises:

*A new heart also will I give you, and a new spirit will I put within you: and I will take away the stony heart out of your flesh, and I will give you an [pink] heart of **flesh*** (Ezekiel 36:26, emphasis added).

The opposite of chaste and modest is lascivious. For instance, a girl in hot-pink shorts may imply passion and lust. Potiphar's wife was probably dressed that way when she tried to tempt Joseph.

The Hidden Meaning of Yellow

ASTLY, WE COME TO *YELLOW*. *Yellow* is an interesting color for several reasons. Like the others, it has several different, though related, meanings. However, the root meaning isn't apparent at first. In fact, it's somewhat hidden.

Of the two times *yellow* is used in the Bible, one is in reference to the plague of leprosy and the other is Psalm 68:13: "Though ye have lain among the pots, yet shall ye be as the wings of a dove covered with silver, and her feathers with yellow gold."

Of course, the dove symbolizes the Holy Spirit. And that gives us the key we need to unlock the hidden meaning of *yellow*. The Holy Spirit is a gift—*yellow* means "gift!" I know the church usually pictures the dove as white, but the Bible doesn't. It describes it as yellow and silver! (*Silver* fits perfectly, too. The *gift* is the Spirit of *Truth*!)

Yellow can also represent the opposite—the devil's evil gifts. God gives us the Comforter; the devil gives us the spirit of fear. A coward is declared to be "yellow," but why? How did *yellow* become associated with fear? The Bible says, "For God hath not *given* us the spirit of fear; but of power, and of love, and of a sound mind" (2 Tim. 1:7, emphasis added). If God has not *given* us the spirit of fear, then where does it come from?

Besides the Holy Spirit, *yellow* can be a symbol for God's other gifts too. One night I dreamed of a yellow rose garden smothered in weeds. I sensed the need for some workers to do the weeding. After I awoke and meditated on what it could mean, God gave me the interpretation. He showed me the church needed more marriage counselors. In this dream, God's gift of marriage was depicted as yellow roses. We usually think of red roses when we think of romance; but the dream's emphasis wasn't romance, but rather the *gift* of marriage. "And Jesus answering said unto them, The children of this world marry, and are *given* in marriage" (Lk. 20:34, emphasis added). And as with every other gift that God gives, He expects us to keep the weeds out of it.

Although of a different type, another gift God has given us is the discerning of spirits (see 1 Cor. 12:10). Once, as I was preparing to teach a seminar for a church where I hadn't ministered before, I had this dream:

> I and a friend named Jim C. walked into a large, strange
> building. We were looking for snakes. Jim said that simply seeing them wasn't sufficient; we had to smell them.

As we walked in, I saw two snakes on my left. I noticed that I couldn't smell them. Both snakes were white in color with light yellow heads. Then I saw two more. I counted four altogether. One snake stood out among the rest. This snake had a large nose like a parrot's beak and it began crawling toward me. I sensed that it could crawl very fast. I asked Jim if it was a parrot beak snake, and he said no, it was a horn nosed snake. As we went further into the building, we saw a meat display case with what I thought were pork chops in it; except these chops were made from cotton mouth snakes instead of pork. Jim picked up one and held it up to show me that it was harmless and good to eat. Then I awoke.

In this dream, Jim C. represents Jesus. He's my friend and instructor throughout the dream, and his initials are a dead giveaway. We were looking for snakes, which represent demons. As the dream clearly revealed, we can't go by what we see (we walk by faith, not by sight); we must smell (discern) them instead. The first *two* snakes indicated the need to judge or discern; their yellow heads referred to a gift, which in this case, portrayed the gift of discerning of spirits. I had trouble smelling them, but Jim didn't. Also, I didn't know what kind of snake the most prominent one was. I thought it was a parrot beak snake, which would be a spirit of deception. (Parrots mimic, and a mimic deceives others by pretending to be something that he's not.) Instead, this snake was a horn nosed snake! A horn represents authority, as does four. (There were four snakes in all.) In other words, God was showing me that the church I was preparing to minister in had a large, swift, witchcraft spirit operating in it.

Then He showed me that I was not to worry. I would not be harmed by the experience, but instead it would be good food for me. Although in the natural, a cotton mouth is very poisonous; when dealing with spiritual serpents, God promised, "Nothing shall by any means hurt you" (Lk. 10:19b).

Even as God admonished Israel when they were about to enter Canaan, God used this dream to admonish me, "Neither fear ye the people of the land; for they are bread [food] for us..." (Num. 14:9b). So, even before I went to this church, I knew what I would encounter when I got there, and I had the promise of victory. After I arrived, although it wasn't clear at first, before long I discerned the spirit which the dream warned me about.

Of course, *yellow* can also warn us of impending danger in the same way that yellow traffic lights caution us to slow down at intersections. And finally, a traditional use of *yellow* is the bright yellow ribbons people attach to their doors and tie to their gate posts to welcome home-comers. I'm not sure where this custom came from, but because it's part of our culture, it shouldn't be ignored when interpreting dreams.

Draw Out the Colors

THEN THERE'S LAVENDER, MAUVE, BEIGE, VIOLET, and dozens more shades and colors that we simply don't have the space in this book to write about. However, if you dream of one, simply apply the same type of reasoning that I've used here. As you meditate, simply ask yourself, "What does this color remind me of? What was I feeling when I dreamed about it?" Often, the answers will be clues. In every case, there's something within the dreamer's own consciousness or experience that will help solve the riddle. Like sweet water from a deep well, it has to be drawn out. "Counsel in the heart of man is like deep water; but a man of understanding will draw it out" (Prov. 20:5).

Chapter Eight

Homing in On God's Will

S EVERAL YEARS AGO I worked as a serviceman for a major appliance company. During that time, I was responsible for an out-of-town service route. Once, I was sent on a service call to a small town in central Louisiana; my directions read, "14 miles from Dry Prong on Highway 167." Since that highway runs north and south through town, I could go either way. When I reached Dry Prong, I stopped and called the dispatcher who originally took the directions and asked for clarification. She said, "Try north." I did, and it was wrong. In fact, I had driven right pass the customer's house on the way into town. Because of her indefinite directions, I drove a total of 56 unnecessary miles that morning before finally finding the correct house.

Vague, imprecise directions not only waste time and resources, they also can be quite frustrating! Trying to do the will of God when you're uncertain as to exactly what it is can be equally frustrating. In Ephesians 5:17 Paul said, "Wherefore be ye not unwise, but understanding what the will of the Lord is." We might think, *Yeah, Paul, that's easy for **you** to say....* Nevertheless, it's obvious that God expects us to know His will, and the only possible way that can happen is if He reveals it to us. So He does. But even though His directions are usually quite precise, they aren't always understood.

He is continually making His will known, using several different methods. One of His favorite methods is dreams. In fact, directions are given in several different forms using many different symbols. Compass directions, right and left turns, and even front and backyards give clear directions once the symbolism contained within them is understood. In this chapter, we will identify directions as they are given in the Bible.

Timing Is Everything

EVERYONE WHO SERVES GOD for any length of time learns that timing is of critical importance when receiving directions. Like the sons of Issachar, we must learn to recognize the signs of the times. Those who know the times lead the race:

> And of the children of Issachar, which were men that had understanding of the times, to know what Israel ought to do; the heads of them were two hundred; and all their brethren were at their commandment (1 Chronicles 12:32).

When interpreting dreams, one of the first questions we should ask ourselves is this: "Is this dream referring to the past, present or future?" To obtain the correct answer, first examine the dream's setting. Where did it take place? What objects or people took part in it? Often the most important key is in the first scene. If its setting is in the past, the dream is probably pointing backward in time. In other words, God is dealing with the dreamer about his past. Past events affect our present circumstances as sure as old spending habits affect our current bank accounts. Before God can change present conditions, sometimes He has to remind us of whatever brought those conditions into existence in the first place.

The Past

SINCE OUR PAST IS BEHIND US, dreaming of something behind us may indicate our past. One's backyard is another simple way of referring to yesterday. Trouble that comes in through the back door is nearly always coming from the past. Although these directions in time are simple, they're often overlooked.

Another purpose God may have for placing something behind someone in a dream is to show that it's lurking there. It may indicate something that's hidden from their view. A back room that is closed up and unused may represent something they're unaware of, but more likely portrays something they're avoiding. Sometimes it's a repressed memory. Some things are just too painful to willfully remember. Therefore, God has to prompt us to bring them to mind so that He can deal with them properly. If God wants to point to one's childhood, He may put the dreamer in his childhood home. When He wants to direct someone even further back, into his distant past, He may place the dreamer in his grandparents' home. Each place indicates a different period of time. In the case of the grandparents' house, it may even imply time before the dreamer was born.

The Future

OBVIOUSLY, THE OPPOSITE of past is future. When a dream refers to one's future, we usually say it's prophetic. In the same way that one's backyard can reflect one's past, one's front yard can predict future events. Sometimes these events are current, already in progress; sometimes they are distant, like the promises in Joseph's dreams.

The Bible also reveals another symbol used in dreams to point forward in time—the morning sun. Each day begins with the sun rising in the east; therefore, an eastward direction may indicate "beginning." (Also, because God gave the Law before He gave grace, *east* can represent the Law. In fact, there are many Scriptures where this holds true.) In the Old Testament, the Hebrew word for *east* is literally "facing the rising sun," or "in front." Herein lies a clue. That which is before, or in front of you, is your future. So if God is speaking of time, an eastward direction may be future tense in the same way that your front yard represents that which is ahead of you.

The Present

BEFORE WE MOVE WESTWARD, let's consider one more thought. Simple deduction says that if the backyard can mean one's past, and the front yard one's future, then one's livingroom may indicate present circumstances. So we have past, present, and future, all illustrated by simple, everyday symbols.

Interpreting the Rooms of Your House

WHILE WE'RE ON THE SUBJECT, let's consider other rooms of the house, including the upper and lower floors. First, our house often represents our self. So the things we do within our house correspond to the things we do within ourselves. We cook up things in the kitchen, which represents our heart. Jesus said:

> *A good man out of the good treasure of the heart bringeth forth good things: and an evil man out of the evil treasure bringeth forth evil things* (Matthew 12:35).

Even more to the point, the Bible makes a direct comparison between an oven and one's heart: "For they have made ready their heart like an oven...in the morning it burneth as a flaming fire" (Hos. 7:6). In like manner, a refrigerator may indicate coldheartedness. Or because we store things in it, it may refer to something tucked away in our memory.

People also store things in the basement, where it's often dark and clammy. This room may portray those deep, dark thoughts we don't want to display in the livingroom, where everyone visits during the day. Likewise, the upper floor corresponds to those lofty thoughts, wonderful intentions, and high praises to God we entertain at other times. Like the one hundred and twenty in the "upper room," it's a good place to have a visitation from God (see Acts 1:13-14). On the other hand, it's not a good place to fall asleep: "And there sat in a window a certain young man named Eutychus, being fallen into a deep sleep...fell down from the third loft, and was taken up dead" (Acts 20:9). Even further, above the upper floor is the attic, which often refers to one's mind or memory—including things put away and long forgotten.

After each day's work, we rest in our bedroom. Likewise, Christians rest in the finished work of Christ at the end of their "day" here on earth. People clean themselves in private, using bathrooms, so a bathroom reflects prayer, such as confession and repentance, because that's the way we dispose of the uncleanness (sins) of the flesh. Along the same line of reasoning, the front porch is open to the public; it shows that which is revealed to all.

When the dream's emphasis is inside versus outside the house, it may be depicting the concept of being included or excluded, or even saved or lost. Christians are inside while sinners are outside. Or as John put it:

> *Blessed are they that do His commandments, that they may have right to the tree of life, and may enter in through the gates into*

the city [house]. *For **without** are dogs, and sorcerers, and whoremongers, and murderers, and idolaters, and whosoever loveth and maketh a lie* (Revelation 22:14-15, emphasis added).

On the other hand, it's better to be outside if there's evil in the house: "It is better to dwell in the wilderness, than with a contentious and an angry woman" (Prov. 21:19).

In any house there are varied and sundry other rooms—guest rooms; sewing rooms; utility rooms; and in some homes, even trophy rooms. Any one of them can represent something important. Both the floor that the room is located on, and each room's purpose, are meaningful. Of course, where the room is located in the dream may not be where it is located in reality. While we're asleep, God can remodel the house to say whatever He wants it to say. Each symbol can teach us something about ourselves and others we live with. By paying close attention, we can "home" in on God's precise instructions for our lives (pun intended). Just how precise God can be is seen in the following dream had by a Christian lady with marital problems:

A tornado hit our home without warning. I watched my husband hang onto the windowsill with all his might. I grabbed my children and ran into our deep closet and waited. After the storm was over, we went out and discovered our house had not been destroyed. All kinds of things had been knocked over, yet the house was in one piece.

This dream warned her of a potentially destructive problem coming against her family. At the same time, it showed her what to do when the storm came. It plainly instructed her to run into her prayer closet and wait upon God (pray!). It also contained a promise of victory—in the end, the home was left intact. In fact, not only was it intact, but in "peace."

Sometimes God may use different parts of the house's construction instead of specific rooms or appliances to give instructions. To illustrate, let's examine the foundations: "If the foundations be destroyed, what can the righteous do?" (Ps. 11:3) A cracked slab is serious, whether it's literal or spiritual. To prevent its destruction in the coming storms, Jesus admonished us to build our spiritual house on the solid rock of His teachings:

> *Whosoever cometh to Me, and heareth My sayings, and doeth them, I will show you to whom he is like: he is like a man which built an house, and digged deep, and laid the foundation on a rock: and when the flood arose, the stream beat vehemently upon that house, and could not shake it: for it was founded upon a rock* (Luke 6:47-48).

Dreaming about the foundational issues of our lives can prevent disaster before problems appear and tear our house apart. Although there are several things that might qualify as "foundational" in our personal lives, when dreaming about the Church, there are only two things specifically declared as foundational in Scripture. One is leadership:

> *Now therefore ye are...of the household of God; and are built upon the foundation of the apostles and prophets, Jesus Christ Himself being the chief corner stone* (Ephesians 2:19-20).

The other is the seven foundation doctrines of the Church:

> *Therefore leaving the principles of the doctrine of Christ, let us go on unto perfection; not laying again the foundation of repentance from dead works, and of faith toward God, of the doctrine of baptisms, and of laying on of hands, and of resurrection of the dead, and of eternal judgment* (Hebrews 6:1-2).

This is God's blueprint for proper construction. Here, the seventh doctrine (perfection) is named first, as it should be. The other six doctrines are listed in correct order for building the house of God.

Stairs are another part of the house that quite often appear in dreams. They may suggest the need to "climb up higher" and take a look in an upper room, or even the attic. Steps may also suggest a process, like the twelve steps of Alcoholics Anonymous.

Windows are another favorite hiding place. Windows can mean anything from revelation knowledge (because they allow light in) to a weakness of our flesh because they provide an opening for the "thief" to get inside (see Joel 2:9). An open window may refer to "a window of opportunity" or it may simply suggest the need to let in some fresh air. In the Bible, a window even became a way of escape for Paul when he was being persecuted: "And through a window in a basket was I let down by the wall, and escaped..." (2 Cor. 11:33). Doors have a similar meaning. Of course, Christ is *the* Door! (see Jn. 10:9)

And lastly, one's office, whether it's within the house, or in separate quarters, may represent one's position or work. It can refer to one's secular job or spiritual ministry. Other items within the home are also meaningful: the washing machine; the iron and ironing board; even the toaster and the burned toast (but we won't go there!). As we've discussed, the number, color, position, and use of each item teaches us something, that is, if we've got ears to hear what it has to say.

How Far Is East From West?

LET'S MOVE ON TOWARD the setting sun. Earlier, I mentioned that *east* means "beginning," and by extension, it can mean the Law. Since the opposite of the Law is grace, one meaning for *west* should be obvious. God said, "As far as the east is from the west, so far hath He removed our transgressions from us" (Ps. 103:12). One might ask, "Just how far is east from west, anyway?" The answer? Let's take a look.

We were destroyed by the Law because it imputed sin unto us (see Rom. 5:13). And even the least sin is fatal: "For whosoever shall keep the whole law, and yet offend in one point, he is guilty of all" (Jas. 2:10).

Now keep in mind that the Law was before grace, as the sun shines in the east before setting in the west. Jesus said, "I am the light of the world..." (Jn. 8:12b)." He is the spiritual light even as the sun is the natural light. At His birth, the Magi came, "Saying, Where is He that is born King of the Jews? for we have seen His star *in the east*" (Mt. 2:2a, emphasis added). He had to arise from the east, because He had to be, "made under the law, to redeem them that were under the law" (Gal. 4:4b-5a). Then, in the same way the sun sets in the west at the end of the day, "in the end of the world...[Jesus] appeared to put away sin by the sacrifice of Himself" (Heb. 9:26b). So the sun rose under the Law, and went down to provide grace. So, how far has He removed our sins from us? Just how far is east from west? As far as the Law is from grace!

Where the Wind Blows

NOW, LET'S LOOK at some scriptural shadows showing the effects of east and west winds (see Heb. 10:1). Keep in mind these shadows were designed to teach us the devastating effects of the Law. Our first shadow is one of Pharaoh's dreams depicting famine: "And, behold, seven thin ears and *blasted with the east wind* sprung up...and...devoured the seven rank and full ears" (Gen. 41:6-7a, emphasis added). The east wind blasted the crop, destroying it. The Law did exactly the same thing to the earth's harvest of souls.

Our second illustration includes one of the many times the Lawgiver Himself cursed Egypt:

> *And Moses stretched forth his rod over the land of Egypt, and the Lord brought an east wind upon the land all that day, and all that night; and when it was morning, the east wind brought the locusts....and they did eat every herb...**and there remained not any green thing** in the trees, or in the herbs of the field, through all the land of Egypt* (Exodus 10:13,15, emphasis added).

It's not hard to see the picture here. The locusts devouring every green thing represents the flesh being destroyed by the Law. But afterward, look at what happened to the locusts:

> *And the Lord turned a mighty strong **west** wind, which took away the locusts, and cast them into the Red sea; there remained not one locust in all the coasts of Egypt* (Exodus 10:19).

Isn't that beautiful? The east wind that cursed the land with locusts represents the spirit of the Law. Paul said the Law is spiritual! But he also said, "For the law of the Spirit of life in Christ Jesus hath made me free from the law of sin and death" (Rom. 8:2). The "Spirit of life" destroyed the locusts. Even the parable of the *Red* sea is superb. God's mighty west wind of grace has removed every destroying law and cast them into the sea of His blood! Not one curse remains! Hallelujah! And this picture was given to us even before Moses gave the Law. God's plan of redemption was finished even before the Law was put into motion.

Lightning From the East

I MENTIONED THAT in the Hebrew language, *east* means "facing the rising sun" or "in front." Therefore, it is similar in meaning to one's front yard—that which is ahead of you. Something that's imminent may come from the east. A prime example is the Lord's return:

> *For as the lightning cometh out of the east, and shineth even unto the west; so shall also the coming of the Son of man be* (Matthew 24:27).

In the natural, lightning may shine from any direction on the compass. But the heavenly display of power we're waiting for only comes from the east. Expectancy is another synonym for this direction.

Go West

E AST MEANS "BEGINNING"; *west* means "end." Similar to *one* and *eleven*, isn't it? Jesus' death was at the end of the age, so by extension *west* can stand for the cross. Revival comes by way of the cross; therefore, west can signify revival:

> *Ask ye of the Lord rain in the time of the latter rain; so the Lord shall make bright **clouds**, and give them **showers** of rain, to every one grass in the field* (Zechariah 10:1, emphasis added).

Those revival showers come right out of the west. Jesus said, "When ye see a *cloud* rise out of the *west*, straightway ye say, There cometh a *shower*; and so it is" (Lk. 12:54b, emphasis added).

The Right and Left Hand of God

E VERYONE KNOWS that a compass needle points north—but not the biblical compass. The Hebrews looked toward the east to orient themselves. Facing east, north is on one's left hand and south is on one's right. These directions are quite significant in the following passage of Scripture:

*When the Son of man shall come in His glory...then shall He sit upon the throne of His glory: and before Him shall be gathered all nations: and He shall separate them one from another, as a shepherd divideth His sheep from the goats: and He shall set the sheep on His **right hand**, but the goats on the **left**. Then shall the King say unto them on His **right hand**, Come, ye blessed of My Father, inherit the kingdom prepared for you from the foundation of the world....Then shall He say also unto them on the **left hand**, Depart from Me, ye cursed, into everlasting fire...* (Matthew 25:31-34,41, emphasis added).

Those who are rejected are placed on His left (north) side. Those who are blessed are set on His right (south). Studying this Scripture, we can see that *right* can mean "accepted," and *left*, "rejected."

Peter said that Jesus is on the right hand of God: "Who is gone into heaven, and is on the right hand of God; angels and authorities and powers being made subject unto Him" (1 Pet. 3:22). Jesus is not only *on* God's right hand, He *is* God's right hand! He's the visible expression of the invisible God: "Thy right hand, O Lord, is become glorious in power: Thy right hand, O Lord, hath dashed in pieces the enemy" (Ex. 15:6). Now if Jesus is on God's right hand, who is on the left? Obviously, God is! God is a spirit. Jesus is both supernatural God and natural man. God, the Spirit, is on the left, or north. Jesus, the man, is on the right, or south. *Left* corresponds to that which is *spiritual* and *right* corresponds to that which is *natural*. This is one of the most important directions given to us through the Word of God.

When someone dreams of making a right-hand turn, God is speaking of a natural change. When one makes a left-hand turn, the change is spiritual. The right turn may involve a job or career change, or even speak of moving to a new location. The spiritual change may mean anything from salvation to a change in attitude.

One of Jesus' "hard sayings" includes this important concept of *right* meaning "natural" and *left* meaning "spiritual." Jesus said:

*But I say unto you, That whosoever looketh on a woman to lust after her hath committed adultery with her already in his heart. And if thy **right eye** offend thee, pluck it out, and cast it from thee: for it is profitable for thee that one of thy members should* *perish, and not that thy whole body should be cast into hell. And if thy **right hand** offend thee, cut if off, and cast it from thee: for it is profitable for thee that one of thy members should perish, and not that thy whole body should be cast into hell* (Matthew 5:28-30, emphasis added).

Have you ever wondered why He emphasized "*right* eye" and "*right* hand"? A man can lust with his left eye, and a left-handed man steals better with his left hand than with his right! *Right* signifies "natural." Jesus is saying if you are consumed with natural lust, pluck it out. Getting rid of your right eye won't solve your problem if you still have your left one. But if you remove the lust, you are free. Likewise, getting rid of covetousness will solve the problem of stealing, while losing your right hand just won't do the job.

God loves puns, and *right* direction may mean *right* choice, or simply correct. For instance, Jesus is on the right side of God. Aren't you glad He's not on the *wrong* side? Another example: *On* the right may mean *in* the right. Besides puns, political views may also be included, as in "far right," "right wing," or "left wing." But I'd better keep going before I get "way out in left field."

Out of the North

JESUS IS ON THE RIGHT SIDE, and God is on the left, or north. The predominate meaning for *north* is "above," in the sense that God is above all. This includes preeminence and sovereignty. God is the judge of all the earth, so a primary extension of *north* is judgment. God's judgment comes out of the north:

*And the word of the Lord came unto me the second time, saying, What seest thou? And I said, I see a seething pot; and the face thereof is toward the **north**. Then the Lord said unto me, **Out of the north** an evil shall break forth upon all the inhabitants of the land* (Jeremiah 1:13-14, emphasis added).

God rules from His throne, which reveals that His throne is on the north side. The devil's attempts to usurp God's throne requires him to ascend to the north:

*For thou hast said in thine heart, I will **ascend** into heaven, I will **exalt** my throne above the stars of God: I will sit also upon* *the mount of the congregation, in the sides of the **north*** (Isaiah 14:13, emphasis added).

God is a spirit, so another branch of *north* is "spiritual." Therefore, *spiritual judgment* is also a legitimate expression for *north*. In the same way that we saw east and west winds can represent the spirits of the Law and grace, a north wind can represent spiritual judgment: "The north wind driveth away rain: so doth an angry countenance a backbiting tongue" (Prov. 25:23).

Down South

CONVERSELY, A SOUTH WIND brings in the natural blessings (or so it would seem). The captain who was given charge of taking Paul to Rome thought so, anyway: "And when the *south wind* blew softly, supposing that they had obtained their purpose, loosing thence, they sailed close by Crete" (Acts 27:13, emphasis added). But were they in for a surprise: "But not long after there arose against it a tempestuous wind, called Euroclydon" (Acts 27:14). Oh well, it was good while it lasted.

North means "above"; *south* means "beneath" or "down." We reflect this in our everyday sayings of "up north" and "down south." When the stock market crashes and businesses fail, we say the market's "gone south." Abraham went down south and got into trouble: "And Abraham journeyed from thence toward the south country..." (Gen. 20:1). Because *south* and *right* are synonymous, *south* can also mean "natural." Natural blessings are real, but short-lived. Paul said the things which are seen won't last:

> *While we look not at the things which are seen, but at the things which are not seen: for the things which are seen are temporal; but the things which are not seen are eternal* (2 Corinthians 4:18).

Abraham's brief problem came from pursuing what he could see with his natural eye instead of what God revealed to him through the spirit. "For [Abraham] looked for a city which hath foundations, whose builder and maker is God" (Heb. 11:10). He may have been looking for a city, but he was looking in the wrong place. He not only got himself in "hot water," he also caused trouble for the king. "But God came to Abimelech in a dream by night, and said to him, Behold, thou art but a dead man, for the woman which thou hast taken; for she is a man's wife" (Gen. 20:3). It didn't take Abraham long to correct his mistake; the king saw to that.

The Right and Left Way

A NOTHER MEANING FOR *RIGHT* is "weakness." *Right* signifies "natural," and natural includes flesh. Jesus said the flesh is *weak!*

> *Watch and pray, that ye enter not into temptation: the spirit indeed is willing, but* **the flesh is weak** *(Matthew 26:41, emphasis added).*

Because man's spirit is ready and willing to serve God, and *left* indicates "spirit," a further extension of *left* is strength. When Solomon built the temple in Jerusalem, he erected two pillars in the porch. When he set up the right pillar, he "called the name thereof Jachin" [he will establish, Heb.]. When he set up the *left*, he "called the name thereof Boaz" [in him is strength, Heb.] (see 1 Kings 7:21).

Paul said, "I can do all things through Christ which strengtheneth me" (Phil. 4:13). God illustrated this in the Old Testament by using left-handed men to do superhuman feats:

> *But when the children of Israel cried unto the Lord, the Lord raised them up a deliverer, Ehud...a Benjamite,* **a man left-handed**: *and by him the children of Israel sent a present unto Eglon the king....And Ehud said, I have* **a message from God** *unto thee....And Ehud put forth his* **left hand**, *and took the dagger from his* **right thigh**, *and thrust it into his belly* (Judges 3:15,20-21, emphasis added).

Ehud carried the dagger on his right thigh because it signified God's message of natural deliverance; however, he stabbed the king with his left hand because his left represented God's anointing.

For most men, the left hand is their weak hand, because the majority are right-handed. God's strength is made perfect in our weakness (left hand). The right hand represents the arm of flesh, or man's strength. As we've already pointed out, Jesus said, "The spirit indeed is willing, but the flesh is weak" (Mt. 26:41b). In other words, of himself, man really doesn't have any strength.

Left can also represent the gifts of the Holy Spirit. To illustrate, let's take a look at some more left-handed Benjamites. First, their ancestor, Benjamin, was Joseph's younger brother. Joseph is a type of Christ. To illustrate: Joseph was his father's favorite son; his brethren turned against him; he was unjustly accused and imprisoned; and finally, he was exalted to Pharaoh's right hand. All of these situations (and more) parallel the life of Jesus. In the same way that Joseph pictures Jesus, Benjamin portrays the Church. Benjamin was found with Joseph's cup, and whoever had Joseph's cup was to become his servant (see Gen. 44:12,17). Likewise, we drink from Jesus' cup and become His servants (see Lk. 22:20).

Jesus' servants are to be like their Master: "The disciple is not above his master: but every one that is perfect shall be as his master" (Lk. 6:40). Jesus knew and accurately revealed the secrets of men's hearts, so we should have the same ability:

> *And the children of Benjamin were numbered....Among all this people there were seven hundred chosen men **lefthanded**; every one could sling stones at an hair breadth, **and not miss*** (Judges 20:15-16, emphasis added).

We shouldn't "miss" either. We're supposed to be able to hit them right between the eyes:

> *But if all prophesy, and there come in one that believeth not, or one unlearned, he is convinced of all, he is judged of all: and thus are the secrets of his heart made manifest; and so falling down on his face he will worship God, and report that God is in you of a truth* (1 Corinthians 14:24-25).

Sounds like the modern church could use a report like that!

A Dream of Direction

SPEAKING OF THE MODERN CHURCH, following is a dream a lady recently had concerning it. (Key words are in italics.):

> In my dream I was on a porch of a rather large house on a hill overlooking a lake. When I glanced out towards the *western* horizon towards the lake, I had a fleeting glimpse of a small tornado. It had *rainbow colors* emanating from it. I crouched on the *porch* (which was on the *west side* of the house) and covered my head, preparing for the wind. I don't recall feeling or hearing the wind. The tornado passed by the house without hurting me or damaging any nearby property.

Next Scene: I was looking out over the lake and saw a large tornado heading towards the house. It was very close. The sky was gray, even though there was a little sunshine. I was calling to the people that were around to take cover, because this tornado was big and moving very fast. It was very windy. I don't recall what everyone else did, but I went *into the house* to take cover. The tornado passed close by the *north* side of the house but again did no damage. As I looked through a *window*, I saw the tornado move towards the *north*, then up into the sky where it broke into many swirling, separate clouds. The clouds then dissipated; the sky quickly cleared and the sun came out.

Even though the clouds cleared and the sun came out, I still sensed danger and that everyone needed to be warned. I called the operator to connect me to the police or fire department to sound the warning sirens. The operator was giving me the run-around and wouldn't connect me to the appropriate emergency personnel. I began urgently raising my voice, saying, "Don't you understand? People need to be warned! The danger isn't over yet!" Then I woke up.

First, the dreamer represents Christians who are watchful and alert to that which is coming upon the earth. Peter said, "For the time is come that judgment must begin at the house of God: and if it first begin at us, what shall the end be of them that obey not the gospel of God?" (1 Pet. 4:17)

This storm comes directly from God, out of the west. Although Christians are subject to His judgment, they're covered by their covenant with God through Jesus Christ. This is represented by the rainbow emanating from the small tornado of His approaching judgment. It's also revealed by the porch. In this context, being on a porch represents being exposed to something while being sheltered at the same time. So the dreamer is exposed to God's judgment but isn't harmed because she is properly covered by her covenant with Him; neither does she feel the wind of His anger.

The second scene isn't quite as comforting. The sunshine represents God's blessings upon the earth at this present time. "God be merciful unto us, and bless us; and cause His face to shine upon us" (Ps. 67:1). It includes the prosperity, freedom, peace, and innumerable other blessings that He has beamed down upon us for so long. The very large, very close storm portrays the impending destruction that He's promised every nation that departs from His grace. "The wicked shall be turned into hell, and all the nations that forget God" (Ps. 9:17).

It moves on the north side and dissipates, but the danger lingers. God is clearly showing the world that His judgments are once again averted by His mercy. Even in the midst of wrath, He remembers mercy, but eventually, His judgments will surely come to pass:

> For the vision is yet for an appointed time, but at the end it shall speak, and not lie: though it tarry, wait for it; because it will surely come... (Habbakuk 2:3).

How much longer before "the big one" touches down? No one knows, but the imminent danger sensed by the dreamer tells us that it's very close. However, like those she tries to warn, few will believe what's coming upon the earth. Revival is our only hope. "O Lord, I have heard Thy speech, and was afraid: O Lord, revive Thy work in the midst of the years, in the midst of the years make known; in wrath remember mercy" (Hab. 3:2). Salvation is the only safe haven. Only those who run "into the house" will have shelter in the coming storm of His fierce judgment.

Also in this dream, the dreamer uses a form of the word *west* twice in the first scene, and *north* twice in the second scene. The first scene is about grace, and the second about impending devastation. As she remembered it, she recorded it. That's important. When recording directions as they appear in dreams, there is one very important concept that everyone should observe. *Don't assume anything.* For instance, if something is on your left hand, don't automatically assume that it's on the north side. In the first place, if you're facing any direction other than east, north is not on the left. Secondly, even if you are facing *east,* and *north* is on your left, *north* and *left* may be closely related, but they don't have the same root meaning. *Left* means "spiritual" and *north* means "above." Also, when you assume something, you wrongly add that assumption to what the dream actually says.

Look at the men who attempted to build the tower of Babel:

*And the whole earth was of one language, and of one speech. And it came to pass, **as they journeyed from the east**, that they found a plain in the land of Shinar....And they said, Go to, let us build us a city and a tower, whose top may reach unto heaven; and let us make us a name...* (Genesis 11:1-2,4, emphasis added).

As you continue reading, you'll discover that although they were traveling "from the east," they definitely weren't heading west! The cross was nowhere in sight. Instead, they were backsliding from God! In this case, *east* clearly represents "beginning."

The Pharisees were coming from the *east* when Jesus confronted them about their selfish views on divorce:

[Jesus] *saith unto them, Moses because of the hardness of your hearts suffered you to put away your wives: but **from the beginning it was not so*** (Matthew 19:8, emphasis added).

They had "journeyed from the east," by departing from the way marriage was in the beginning. Those who were attempting to build the tower of Babel were doing the same.

Three Views of the Cross

SUMMARIZING THE BIBLE'S UNIQUE COMPASS, the Hebrew orients himself by facing the *eastern* sun, which symbolizes his adherence to the Law in his vain attempt to make a place for himself with God. On his right hand, toward the *south*, lies his natural, temporal blessings. On his left, to the *north*, judgment impatiently awaits like a hungry vulture perched atop a barren tree. If he repents and turns fully around and faces the *western* Son, he beholds the end purpose of the Law which he has struggled to obey (see 2 Cor. 3:13; Gal. 3:24). When he lays down his dead, religious works and takes up his cross, he finally discovers what it really means to be a true son of Abraham.

The *northward* bound, unbelieving Gentile glances at his compass to assure himself that he is indeed racing toward the judgment bar of Almighty God. "As it is appointed unto men once to die, but after this the judgment" (Heb. 9:27). If, in his attempts to escape destruction he turns *eastward*, to his *right* in self-righteousness, trusting in the arm of the flesh, he usually becomes beguiled and misguided by the map of religious tradition and formalism. As he approaches mid-life and finds himself in a crisis, he may turn and *go south* toward the pleasures of this world. There, he shall surely perish. But, if he comes to himself and heeds the gentle call of God's precious Spirit, he will make a spiritual turn to the left and find his place in the *western*, setting Son. There, Christ "ever lives to make intercession" for him, and there, at the end of the day, he finds rest from his own futile efforts at righteousness (see Heb. 7:25).

On the other hand, the Christian orients himself by facing *westward*, steadfastly looking to the cross of Jesus Christ as the power of his salvation (see 1 Cor. 1:18). Forgetting the *eastern* Law which is forever behind him, "and reaching forth unto those things which are before, [he] press[es] toward the mark for the prize of the high calling of God in Christ Jesus" (Phil. 3:13b-14). By faith, he earnestly searches "for a city which hath foundations, whose builder and maker is God" (Heb. 11:10). He knows that it's located somewhere to the *north*, on his right because his guide book, the Holy Bible, declares that, "Beautiful for situation, the joy of the whole earth, is mount Zion, on the sides of the north, the city of the great King" (Ps. 48:2). He disdains to go *south*, which lies to his left, toward a world which has rejected its Savior. But he knows that if he was to make a mistake and get lost, he need only turn and look toward the setting Son. There, His loving Savior always beckons the way back home.

From this simple, threefold picture, you can see that it's not the direction in which you look that determines the meaning of what you see. Rather it's your perspective, determined by where you're coming from. Your viewpoint is what's important. We each have the land before us. We each have to make our own choice:

*And the Lord said unto Abram, after that Lot was separated from him, Lift up now thine eyes, and look **from the place where thou art** northward, and southward, and eastward, and westward: for all the land which thou seest, to thee will I give it, and to thy seed for ever (Genesis 13:14-15; emphasis added).*

Chapter Nine

All Creatures Great and Small

WHEN GOD CREATED the world's inhabitants, He first made the birds and fish, and then progressed to land animals. All in all, Genesis lists five different types of creatures that He made. Although His animal creation included every creepy-crawly thing in existence, He mentions only a few by name. We'll keep our discussion down to a few, also.

It wasn't until the fifth day that God made living, moving creatures, and that gives us a clue as to what animals were made for: They were all created to serve Him. (Remember, *five* means "service.") This information also helps us to see how creatures are used as symbols. So let's take a look at the Genesis record:

And God said, Let the waters bring forth abundantly the moving creature that hath life, and fowl that may fly above the earth in the open firmament of heaven. And God created great whales, and every living creature that moveth, which the waters brought forth abundantly, after their kind, and every winged fowl after his kind: and God saw that it was good. And God blessed them, saying, Be fruitful, and multiply, and fill the waters in the seas, and let fowl multiply in the earth. And the evening and the morning were the fifth day. And God said, Let the earth bring forth the living creature after his kind, cattle, and creeping thing, and beast of the earth after his kind: and it was so. And God made the beast of the earth after his kind, and cattle after their kind, and every thing that creepeth upon the earth after his kind: and God saw that it was good. And God said, Let us make man in our image, after our likeness: and let them have dominion over the fish of the sea, and over the fowl of the air, and over the cattle, and over all the earth, and over every creeping thing that creepeth upon the earth. So God created man in his own image, in the image of God created he him; male and female created he them. And God blessed them, and God said unto them, Be fruitful, and multiply, and replenish the earth, and subdue it: and have dominion over the fish of the sea, and over the fowl of the air, and over every living thing that moveth upon the earth (Genesis 1:20-28).

The Fish of the Sea

THE WATERS BROUGHT FORTH the fish and fowl. Water often depicts things that are spiritual, and because the fish and fowl were brought forth from water, their source reveals they relate to spiritual things—especially things that relate to the soul. For instance, Jesus used *fish* as a type of *lost* souls. He said to Peter and Andrew, "Follow Me, and I will make you fishers of men" (Mt. 4:19b). We know that most symbols have opposite meanings; and so, *fish* can also represent souls that are saved. After all, one doesn't cease to be a fish just because he's been caught! Now there are several different kinds of fish: big fish, little fish, cute fish, ugly fish, dangerous fish, schooling fish...the list goes on and on. So rather than trying to identify each particular fish and its symbolic meaning, we'll discuss different groups of fish and what they portray. However, let's first examine one fish specifically mentioned in the Bible.

A Naked Scavenger

CLEARLY IDENTIFIABLE FROM ITS DESCRIPTION in the Bible is the catfish. Now I love to eat catfish, but under Moses Law, like many other delectable foods, they were forbidden: "And whatsoever hath not fins and scales ye may not eat; it is unclean unto you" (Deut. 14:10). Although catfish have fins, they don't have scales. Now why did God single them out like that?

The answer is although most creatures are covered with something—scales, feathers, hair, or even clothes in the case of man—catfish are as naked as the day they were born (or hatched, I should say). Because catfish are uncovered, they were declared unclean under Moses' Law. This reveals that we are also unclean when uncovered. Because most of us wear clothes, we consider ourselves to be covered. God thinks otherwise. When Adam and Eve made themselves aprons out of fig leaves, God said, "That just won't do!" (Well, not exactly, but close.) He made fur coats for them instead. Of course, something had to die before it would share its hide with Adam, so God killed it. That is the message. That's the central theme of the entire Bible. Jesus had to die to cover us with His blood, or we would still be unclean in the sight of God.

Now there is one more characteristic of catfish that makes them forbidden under the Law. They are scavengers. They feed right off the bottom of the lake. God does not want us to eat from the off-scouring of this world. He wants us to feast on the Bread of Life. So the catfish is a miniature picture of a sinner feeding on filth. Of course, if you dream that you catch one, it may represent a sinner saved by the grace of God. Hmm...then maybe the gospel could be compared to the hook, line, and sinker that he swallowed, right? Or, maybe the net?

Every Creeping Thing

CATFISH AREN'T THE ONLY FISH forbidden by the Law. So are crawfish. Or, if you don't eat crawfish, what about shrimp or lobster? They're all in the same boat. Moses didn't call them by name, but they are all considered forbidden foods. Now, what did they do to deserve that? They just have too many feet, and besides that, they "creep" around:

> *And every creeping thing that creepeth upon the earth shall...not be eaten....or whatsoever hath more [than four] feet among all creeping things that creep upon the earth, them ye shall not eat...* (Leviticus 11:41-42).

God just doesn't like creeps! For that matter, I'm not too fond of them either. Now, since the ordinances of the Law have been removed, all these things are acceptable table fare, but the message they were made to teach still applies.

Notice that all three of these crustaceans—crawfish, shrimp, and lobster—also feed off the bottom, like catfish. Besides the obvious picture that fact reveals, crawfish are also famous for "crawfishing" their way out of uncomfortable situations (like we all have a tendency to do at one time or another.) And shrimp? Just like their name implies, they're just too small for the job. Now lobster, they're different. They belong on a king's table! They're much too expensive for poor people to eat. They're part of the lifestyle of the rich and famous. That may explain how they got on God's rejected list. Of course, they can represent His blessings too. After all, we are children of the King!

Clean or Unclean

THERE ARE QUITE A FEW MORE unclean creatures on God's list of "Thou shalt not eat..." but usually it's not difficult to see why He made each one. The individual characteristics of each one reflect some aspect of man. Creatures that Moses listed as unclean portray a host of evil things:

> *Now the works of the flesh are evident, which are: adultery, fornication, uncleanness, lewdness, idolatry, sorcery, hatred, contentions, jealousies, outbursts of wrath, selfish ambitions, dissensions, heresies, envy, murders, drunkenness, revelries, and the like; of which I tell you...that those who practice such things will not inherit the kingdom of God (Galatians 5:19-20 NKJ).*

> *Mortify therefore your members which are upon the earth...inordinate affection, evil concupiscence, and covetousness, which is idolatry....[and] also put off all these; anger, wrath, malice, blasphemy, filthy communication out of your mouth. Lie not one to another, seeing that ye have put off the old man with his deeds (Colossians 3:5,8-9).*

And there's more, but that's enough for you to get the idea. God probably made a specific creature to represent each and every one of these unclean things. Or is it the other way around? I've seen several carnivorous souls that reminded me of piranhas. And who wouldn't recognize a loan shark? Or what about an octopus taking a pretty girl out on her first date?

And, as always, there's a flip side. God created many clean creatures, too. As long as a fish was covered and had fins, it was considered fine table fare. In dreams, *fish* not only represent souls, but they can also stand for the Holy Spirit:

> *If a son shall ask bread of any of you that is a father, will he give him a stone? or if he ask a **fish**, will he for a **fish** give him a serpent?...If ye then, being evil, know how to give good gifts unto your children: how much more shall your heavenly Father give the **Holy Spirit** to them that ask Him?* (Luke 11:11-13, emphasis added)

If *fish* can represent the Holy Spirit, common sense says they can also represent unholy spirits. In fact, it's usually unclean spirits which produce, "the motions of sins, which...work in our members to bring forth fruit unto death" (Rom. 7:5).

Besides souls, the Holy Spirit, and unclean spirits, *fish* can also manifest the hidden motives of the heart. Some *fish* are clever predators; they disguise themselves to deceive their unaware prey. God's fishermen must also be clever. "He that winneth souls is wise" (Prov. 11:30). Soul fishing is always a waiting game. It doesn't pay to get impatient or lose hope. Asking the right questions when you're fishing for answers helps fill your creel too; it's like baiting your hook with just the right bait. And if you can stand one more pun, you *must* have the right *line* if you expect to catch anything.

A Bird's Eye View

NOW LET'S ASCEND UP HIGHER and get a bird's eye view of this picture. In the same way that God declared some fish were clean and others weren't, He also considered birds to be clean or unclean. When I first started preaching, I was guilty of the same mistake that most young preachers make—oversimplification. (That's a kind way of saying narrow-minded.) I used to teach that the Law only commanded us not to do things that we would naturally do. I didn't think God would forbid something that we weren't going to do anyway. But I was wrong.

Another Naked Scavenger

TO ILLUSTRATE MY POINT, let me ask you a question. Have you ever been tempted to eat buzzard? Me neither! But they were forbidden as food under Moses' Law. Now it's not difficult to understand why God would say, "Thou shalt not covet." Likewise, everyone has been tempted to lie at one time or another. But why in the world would God command us not to put buzzard on the table? This is one of the clearest pictures in the Bible showing us that the Law is spiritual, rather than carnal. God wasn't giving Israel a set of dietary rules; He was teaching them to discern the difference between acceptable and unacceptable behavior. The lesson of the buzzard is exactly the same one as the catfish—both are uncovered and both are scavengers. Because buzzards are creatures of the air instead of water, they reflect man's spirit instead of his soul.

A buzzard is a perfect picture of a seemingly spiritual person who isn't under authority. Feathers cover his body, but nothing covers his head:

> *But I would have you know, that the head of every man is Christ; and the head of the woman is the man; and the head of Christ is God* (1 Corinthians 11:3).

If you are in rebellion, you're unclean. If you're not under authority, you're a buzzard in God's sight, even if you can soar in the heavenly realms! Truly spiritual people aren't scavengers either. They won't eat things like pride and prejudice; envy and jealousy; hatred and anger; because all those things are buzzard bait. They're roadkill.

Birds of the Night

THERE ARE SEVERAL MORE forbidden birds on Moses' list. And just as you detest buzzards (or if you're from the city, vultures), you probably won't like these either! You'll find the complete list in Leviticus 11:13-19. For our purposes we'll name only a few of them. The first one is the owl. Owls are birds of the night. Paul said, "Ye are all the children of light, and the children of the day: we are *not of the night*, nor of darkness" (1 Thess. 5:5, emphasis added).

So, like catfish and buzzards, owls may stand for sinners or unclean spirits. On the other hand, an owl may represent one who is skillful in discerning of spirits because of its acute vision and hearing. These wonderful characteristics aid them in the night, making them expert hunters even in almost total darkness.

I'm sure someone reading this book is going to think, *I thought owls meant wisdom?* Everyone has heard the saying, "He's a wise old owl." Right! There are times when they do mean wisdom. Jesus said, "The children of this world are in their generation wiser than the children of light" (Lk. 16:8b). As with every symbol, an *owl* may represent either good or evil, which is determined by the dream's content, not by the fact that an owl is an owl. God didn't make any bad creatures; however, He did create some to represent evil. He said everything that He made was *"very good"* (see Gen. 1:31). Paul, in reference to clean and unclean things said, "There is nothing unclean of itself..." (Rom. 14:14b).

In fact, even a vulture can represent something good. Jesus used them to represent angels in a parable about the resurrection. "For wheresoever the carcase is, there will the eagles [vultures, Greek] be gathered together" (Mt. 24:28). There are few dead carcases that vultures can't find. As they circle overhead, their acute sense of smell enables them to locate the dead even when the carcase isn't visible from the sky. Jesus used their unique ability to assure us that not a single dead person would be overlooked in the resurrection.

Birds of Prey

BESIDES VULTURES AND OWLS, eagles and fish hawks are also on Moses' list. Both of these predators feed on fish. God doesn't like competition. He said, "All souls are mine" (Ezek. 18:4a). He doesn't like sharing His "fish" with spiritual predators. One of the most vivid and memorable dreams I've ever had was about a hawk:

> I dreamed that I was looking out my window and saw a hawk alight in a tree. I was using a pair of binoculars, but at first, I couldn't get them to focus properly. Then, when they suddenly came into focus, I realized the hawk had a man's head! I watched him spread his wings and drop to the ground. As he landed, he became a well-dressed man. He was wearing a suit. He looked toward me and realized I was watching him. He knew that if he walked away, he would look suspicious, so he walked toward me instead.

He came into the house, and at this point, I saw that he was carrying a shotgun. The gun was beautifully engraved and inlaid with gold.

As he entered the house, I asked, "Hunting quail?" His reply was unintelligible so I repeated the question, but I knew that in reality he was "a hunter of the souls of men." He nodded affirmative to my question, and I asked him if I could examine his shotgun. I placed it to my shoulder and noticed that the action wasn't properly fitted to the stock. It looked impressive, but it wasn't very powerful. I also noticed that it was foreign made. I handed it back to him and told him that it needed repairs. I said, "You'd better take that gun to a good gunsmith; it's dangerous." Then I awoke.

Three years passed before I met this hawk. And just like the dream depicted, at first I didn't recognize him for what he really was. When I finally focused in on him, I realized that he was a sorcerer, although he had every appearance of being a "well-dressed" preacher. He was hunting souls, but he wasn't hunting them for God's glory; he was hunting them for his own. His speech was eloquent and his teachings were beautiful, but forged in a foreign land. His doctrines came straight from the pits of hell. His purpose was to draw away disciples after himself. He was indeed an evil hunter of the souls of men.

In addition to hawks, there are several more fish-eating birds forbidden under Moses' Law: cormorants, pelicans, and herons, to name a few. When used in a context like the dream above, they each portray the wrong spirit.

Earlier, I mentioned that eagles were also forbidden to eat. Yet God uses eagles as a type of the prophetic anointing. Compare, "And by a prophet the Lord brought Israel out of Egypt, and by a prophet was he preserved" (Hos. 12:13), with, "Ye have seen what I did unto the Egyptians, and how I bare you on eagles' wings, and brought you unto Myself" (Ex. 19:4). Here, God uses the eagle's unique characteristic of carrying her young on her back as a picture of His powerful deliverance of Israel from slavery in Egypt. He refers to it again in this Scripture:

As an eagle stirreth up her nest, fluttereth over her young, spreadeth abroad her wings, taketh them, beareth them on her wings: so the Lord alone did lead him, and there was no strange god with him (Deuteronomy 32:11-12).

In this Scripture He even compares the eagle to Himself. So, like the lowly, unclean catfish, the lofty, majestic eagle can represent both the clean and the unclean, depending upon its use in one's dream.

Another one of the eagle's characteristics is seen in Psalm 103:5: "Who satisfieth thy mouth with good things; so that thy youth is renewed like the eagle's." Here the reference is to the eagle's seasonal molting and renewing its plumage. No doubt that's what is meant in this next Scripture too:

But they that wait upon the Lord shall renew their strength; they shall mount up with wings as eagles; they shall run, and not be weary; and they shall walk, and not faint (Isaiah 40:31).

Creatures of the Night

BIRDS HAVE SEVERAL UNIQUE CHARACTERISTICS that enable them to be used in many different roles in dreams. In addition to being able to fly, they're very colorful; their habits and habitat are varied; they walk on two legs; and they are the only creatures with feathers. But they are not the only ones that fly. Bats fly too. Bats are different from birds in many respects, yet they are similar in that they have only two legs and can fly. Like owls, they are creatures of the night. They're also on Moses' list of forbidden foods. One species is called vampire bats because they drink blood. This, along with all their other faults, makes them a perfect symbol for witchcraft, and that is usually what they signify. There are a few more things they can represent, like near blindness, giving rise to the expression, "Blind as a bat." Bats usually portray something negative. In fact, it's hard to imagine them being used any other way. But they have one redeeming trait—they invented radar (well almost, anyway). A bat uses sound as a type of radar to fly in complete darkness. This is comparable to discerning of spirits, one of the nine spiritual gifts given to the Church.

Multitude of Meanings

THERE ARE SEVERAL MORE SCRIPTURES where birds are used symbolically. In the following passage, evil is symbolized by a restless raven and rest and peace by a dove:

> And [Noah] *sent forth a raven* [from the ark], *which went forth to and fro, until the waters were dried up from off the earth. Also he sent forth a dove....But the dove found no rest for the sole of her foot, and she returned unto him into the ark.... And he stayed yet other seven days; and again he sent forth the dove out of the ark; and the dove came in to him in the evening; and, lo, in her mouth was an olive leaf plucked off: so Noah knew that the waters were abated from off the earth. And he stayed yet other seven days; and sent forth the dove; which returned not again unto him any more* (Genesis 8:7-12).

Thousands of years later Isaiah wrote, "But the wicked are like the troubled sea, when it cannot rest" (Is. 57:20), and a thousand years after that, Jesus interpreted Noah's actions:

> And into whatsoever house ye enter, first say, Peace be to this house. And if the son of peace be there, your peace shall rest upon it: if not, it shall turn to you again (Luke 10:5-6).

Birds can also represent gossip and slander as seen in the following Scripture: "Curse not the king, no not in thy thought; and curse not the rich in thy bedchamber: for a bird of the air shall carry the voice, and that which hath wings shall tell the matter" (Eccles. 10:20). Why, the little tattletale! They can also represent the cause, or spirit, behind a curse: "As the bird by wandering, as the swallow by flying, so the curse causeless shall not come" (Prov. 26:2).

Beasts, Cattle, and Creeping Things

AS THE SIXTH DAY OF CREATION DAWNED, God undertook another momentous task, the formation of land animals:

> And God made the beast of the earth after his kind, and cattle after their kind, and every thing that creepeth upon the earth after his kind: and God saw that it was good (Genesis 1:25).

Notice there are three specific classifications mentioned here: *beast, cattle,* and *creeping things.* They are three important keys to understanding the symbolism hidden in animals.

An elder who was quite concerned about a distressing situation in his church was earnestly seeking God for help:

> He dreamed that a dangerous bear was approaching him. Suddenly a giant snake appeared between him and the bear. The snake killed and ate the bear, swallowing him whole in the process. Then the serpent turned toward the elder, becoming a huge gorilla in the process. The startled elder awoke in fear.

Earlier we introduced Elisha's bears that mauled forty-two scornful kids, and showed that they represented a curse. The Bible teaches that a serpent may also be a curse:

> *And the Lord God said unto the serpent, Because thou hast done this, **thou art cursed** above all cattle, and above every beast of the field; upon thy belly shalt thou go, and dust shalt thou eat all the days of thy life* (Genesis 3:14, emphasis added).

In the elder's dream, one curse devoured another! That's exactly what the gospel is all about! "Christ hath redeemed us from the curse of the law, being made a curse for us: for it is written, Cursed is every one that hangeth on a tree" (Gal. 3:13). After dying to atone for our sins, destroying the curse that we were under in the process, Jesus arose to walk in the power of an endless life. Thus He became the "stronger than he" of Luke 11:21-22:

> *When a strong man armed keepeth his palace, his goods are in peace: but when a stronger than he shall come upon him, and overcome him, he taketh from him all his amour wherein he trusted, and divideth his spoils.*

A gorilla is the "strong man" of the forest, even as Christ is the "strong man" of His creation. Through this dream, God was assuring the elder that He had indeed intervened on his behalf, and through the cross of Christ, had completely resolved his threatening problem.

This dream clearly illustrates two of the three classifications of land creatures mentioned above. A *beast* is a creature that dominates. For example, "A lion which is strongest among beasts, and turneth not away for any" (Prov. 30:30). As one can see from this dream, these animals represent danger, power, strength, leadership, and other similar characteristics. The serpent is one of the *creepy creatures*. The Hebrew word translated *creep* actually means "to glide swiftly," like a serpent slithering through the grass. They are sneaky. This corresponds to everything from wisdom to witchcraft. In contrast, *cattle* are gregarious animals and represent the social aspect of mankind. They follow the leader.

The Beast of the Earth

THE BEAST CATEGORY INCLUDES the anti-Christ of John's vision:

> *And I stood upon the sand of the sea, and saw a **beast** rise up out of the sea, having seven heads and ten horns, and upon his horns ten crowns, and upon his heads the name of blasphemy* (Revelation 13:1, emphasis added).

On the other hand, the beast category also includes John's vision of Christ's ministers in the King's throne room:

> *And before the throne there was a sea of glass like unto crystal: and in the midst of the throne, and round about the throne, were four beasts full of eyes before and behind. And the first beast was like a lion, and the second beast like a calf, and the third beast had a face as a man, and the fourth beast was like a flying eagle* (Revelation 4:6-7).

The lion represents the apostles; the calf (or ox) portrays the evangelists; the man depicts the pastor-teachers; and as we have already seen, the eagle represents the prophets.

There are several animals named in the Bible that are beasts of burden. They all belong to the same category as cattle. Some are considered clean, and others unclean. Interestingly enough, the difference has nothing to do with whether they're tame and useful, or even whether they're good table fare, but instead it depends upon what they wear on their feet and how they eat! Moses' only concern was whether their hooves were solid or divided, and whether they chewed a cud or not:

> *Whatsoever parteth the hoof, and is clovenfooted, and cheweth the cud, among the beasts, that shall ye eat. Nevertheless these shall ye not eat of them that chew the cud, or of them that divide the hoof: as the camel, because he cheweth the cud, but divideth not the hoof; he is unclean unto you* (Leviticus 11:3-4).

The latter part of this Scripture is another one of those buzzard laws. I don't think I'd care for camel meat anyway; what about you?

The writer of Hebrews said the Law had "a shadow of good things to come, and not the very image of the things..." (Heb. 10:1b). Paul compared the Law to a bronze mirror, which produces a somewhat dim and distorted reflection (see 1 Cor. 13:12). The Law governing clean and unclean creatures contains many obscure pictures such as they describe. Let's take a closer look at some of these clouded images.

Dividing the Hoof and Chewing the Cud

D IVIDING THE HOOF relates to "rightly dividing the word" (see 2 Tim. 2:15); in the spirit, we walk with our words. Adam and Eve "heard the voice of the Lord God walking in the garden." (Gen. 3:8a). That's the reason God said you should have "your feet shod with the preparation of the gospel of peace" (Eph. 6:15). That's also the meaning of the strange custom described in Ruth:

> *Now this was the manner in former time in Israel concerning redeeming and concerning changing, for* **to confirm all things; a man plucked off his shoe, and gave it to his neighbour:** *and this was a testimony in Israel* (Ruth 4:7, emphasis added).

Giving another person one's shoe was the same as saying, "I give you my word."

Whether you dream of hooves or shoes, they mean the same thing—*words*. And since we walk with words, by extension *walk* is another meaning for feet and shoes. Moses' Law reveals that those who try to use God's Word without correctly dividing it are considered unclean (in error) in the eyes of God. Dividing the Word is what we're doing right now. We're dividing the natural ordinances to obtain the spiritual meanings. In other words, we're separating the natural from the spiritual. And the way we're doing it is by chewing the cud. That's what meditating upon the Word is all about. We have to "chew on it awhile" before we can grasp the underlying thought behind some of its hard sayings. Through meditation, we break them down until we comprehend their true meaning. Then, once we understand them, we can do what they instruct us to do, utilizing them to direct our lives. Otherwise, we're just swallowing the Word whole without benefiting from it.

Bulls and Oxen

DREAMING OF AN ANIMAL with hooves, divided or otherwise, doesn't necessarily mean the animal refers to words. There are several more characteristics that should be taken into consideration. For example, bulls often have horns, and are known for aggression. *Horns* mean "power" and "authority," but not necessarily legitimate authority. Quite often a bull symbolizes opposition and persecution. Another meaning is idolatry, or by extension, it can stand for false religion. When the stock market is involved, a bull refers to prosperity. Occasionally, it means the same as when a person says, "That's just a bunch of bull."

On the flip side, when Paul was defending his apostleship to the Corinthians, he used *oxen* symbolically to represent God's ministers: "For it is written in the law of Moses, Thou shalt not muzzle the mouth of the ox that treadeth out the corn..." (1 Cor. 9:9), especially the evangelistic aspect of the ministry, "...that he that ploweth should plow in hope; and that he that thresheth in hope should be partaker of his hope" (1 Cor. 9: 10). Why are oxen used to depict ministers? For three specific reasons.

First, oxen are neutered animals. Evangelists are not supposed to gather for themselves, but for God. The Church is the King's harem, not the evangelist's nor the pastor's. Ministers are to be spiritual eunuchs in the house of their God. Second, oxen are used for sowing and reaping. As Paul mentioned in the Scripture above, the ox was the primary animal used for plowing and threshing. Third, oxen are used to depict ministers because increase in the Body of Christ is by their labors: "Where no oxen are, the crib is clean: but much increase is by the strength of the ox" (Prov. 14:4).

A Hog of Himself

OXEN HAVE A DIVIDED HOOF, and chew the cud; therefore, they are clean. On the other hand, hogs have divided hoofs, but are considered unclean. Everyone knows that pork is one of Moses' forbidden foods. But like catfish, they taste mighty good! So why is pork declared unclean? Hogs don't chew the cud. We've already discussed the spiritual picture behind cud chewing and what it signifies, but there are a couple more reasons that hogs wouldn't have qualified anyway. When a pig eats, he always makes a "hog of himself." Really, they are gluttons. They have to be. Unlike other land creatures that depend upon their fur for warmth, they must depend upon their fat. Although they do have some hair, it is completely insufficient to "cover" them. So they eat everything they can to provide a surplus layer of fat for protection. They're just like unsaved rich people. Their covering is their surplus, not their God. They trust in their riches: "Jesus...saith unto them, Children, how hard is it for *them that trust in riches* to enter into the kingdom of God!" (Mk. 10:24b, emphasis added). Also, like catfish and vultures, hogs are scavengers. So we have three unclean creatures: swine on the land, catfish in the sea, and vultures in the air representing the unclean aspects of man's body, soul, and spirit.

A Horse of a Different Color

ANOTHER DOMESTICATED ANIMAL determined to be unclean under the Law is the horse. Moses declared them unclean because their hooves aren't divided, but that doesn't keep Jesus from riding on one. He rode into Jerusalem on a donkey, but He'll be riding a warhorse when He returns for His next visit:

> *And I saw heaven opened, and behold a white horse; and He that sat upon him was called Faithful and True, and in righteousness He doth judge and make war. His eyes were as a flame of fire, and on His head were many crowns....and His name is called The Word of God* (Revelation 19:11-13).

Horses have been used for work, war, and transportation for centuries. Two of these three categories usually determine how they're used in dreams. Although they were the primary means of transportation for centuries, they have been replaced in modern times with "horseless carriages"—automobiles. But in many parts of the world, they are still used as draft animals. Also, as in the Scripture above, *horses* can still mean war. Their courage, speed, and stamina have made them invaluable war allies throughout history.

As we learned when we discussed colors, there are four horses in the sixth chapter of Revelation. The first was white, the second red, the third black, and the fourth pale. Purity, persecution, famine, and death—each rider carried a message from God. There is one more factor that enters into the interpretation of their messages—*time*. Their messages were consecutive. Each horse represented a specific period of time.

I once dreamed of thirteen evil women, riding thirteen black horses in the middle of the night. When I awoke, I asked God what in the world that was all about and He said, "Thirteen evil weeks." And indeed they were. I had exactly thirteen weeks left on my job before we moved, and those thirteen weeks gave new meaning to Jesus' words, "Take therefore no thought for the morrow: for the morrow shall take thought for the things of itself. *Sufficient unto the day is the evil thereof*" (Mt. 6:34, emphasis added).

After that, at another time, in another state, I dreamed of four horses. The first two were strong, beautiful, quarter horses. The third was like the first two, but as I passed by, he lifted up his heel, threatening to kick me. The fourth was a lean, mean, red horse that opposed me and tried to bite me as I attempted to pass by him. Because I had been introduced to the concept of time as it related to horses in my previous dream, I knew exactly what God was saying. He was giving me advanced insight into the next four weeks of ministry. I called several ministers whom I was working with and explained the dream to them. I warned them that toward the end of the third week we would be threatened, and the fourth would be curtains. It came to pass just as the dream depicted. The first two and a half weeks were unusually productive; but toward the end of the third week, the devil raised his ugly head. By the beginning of the fourth, we were facing stiff opposition and by its end, total rejection. I left then; enough is enough!

Now, hold your horses. Don't think that I'm teaching that every horse you dream about means exactly one week in time; rather *one* of the meanings for a *horse* is a specific period of time.

That time period may be any length that God assigns to it, not just one week as in my dreams. In fact, each rider of the four horses of Revelation rode for a different length of time. The white horse represented the Church's expansion and rapid growth for the first hundred years or so. The red horse ran longer, for the Saints were persecuted sporadically until 325 AD. The black horse had the most stamina of all, because he started his race about 325 AD and he didn't tire out for over a thousand years. It wasn't until about the time of Martin Luther that he was sent back to the barn. And, if the pale horse's two riders, death and hell, had stayed in the saddle much longer, it would have spelled curtains for the whole human race. They managed to destroy one-fourth of the world's population as it was. Their ride coincides with the era of the bubonic plague, or the black death as it was called (see Rev. 6:1-8).

Now war, work, and time, by themselves, aren't the only things to consider when you dream about horses. The common term, *horsepower*, involves work and time together. The two are inseparable. If God uses a horse to refer to your work, He usually has time in mind also. A similar and somewhat related meaning is seen in the word *horseflesh*. The emphasis here is flesh, or the *works of the flesh*, when the two are combined. So war, work, and time, sometimes individually, sometimes entwined, are some of the things that horses convey in our dreams.

One more thought, the white horse of John's vision in Revelation 6:2 is a type of the Holy Spirit. And besides the Holy Spirit, a horse may symbolize our own spirit as well. Like people, some horses are quite "spirited," while others are just worn-out old nags.

Countless Creature Characteristics

UNDER THE LAW, if a creature had more than four feet, wasn't covered with fur, feathers, or scales, and had solid hooves, it was unclean. Also, even if its hooves were divided, if it didn't chew the cud, it was still considered unclean. But these weren't the only criteria for judging uncleanness. Moses listed several more creatures as unclean without giving any specific reason. Usually, one can determine the reason by examining the inherent characteristics of the unclean animal. For example, we've seen several reasons that hogs are on God's unclean list, but there's one more reason.

Hogs don't have sweat glands. That's why they're always wallowing in the mud. They can't rid themselves of their body heat any other way. Dogs are similar, except dogs pant when they get hot. What's the picture here? Heat is passion. When men wallow in the filth of this world to relieve their passions ("body heat"), they are as unclean swine. When they rid themselves of their anger and frustrations through swearing and cursing, they pant like dogs and offend God with their sin:

> *But above all things, my brethren, swear not, neither by heaven, neither by the earth, neither by any other oath: but let your yea be yea; and your nay, nay; lest ye fall into condemnation* (James 5:12).

Of course, dogs will bite the hand that feeds them, too. They often represent strife in dreams. Solomon said, "He that passeth by, and meddleth with strife belonging not to him, is like one that taketh a dog by the ears" (Prov. 26:17).

The Bible never speaks well of dogs, unless you commend them for eating Jezebel (see 1 Kings 21:23). But occasionally, they are used in a positive sense in our dreams. Many cultures consider a dog to be man's best friend, and guard dogs can even represent God's ministers who are faithfully watching for the welfare of the Saints. They can also represent the not-so-faithful:

> *His watchmen are blind: they are all ignorant, they are all dumb dogs, they cannot bark; sleeping, lying down, loving to slumber* (Isaiah 56:10).

Cats are closely akin to dogs in that both are common house pets; however, they have a completely different meaning. Cats are fiercely independent. They have a mind of their own. They are associated with witchcraft in many fairy tales, and sometimes that's what they stand for in dreams. A cat can represent several other spirits, too. I was traveling with another minister several years ago when one night he dreamed that he was watering his cat. In the process, he almost drowned it. He said the cat looked pitiful. He woke up feeling sorry for it. When he asked me what I thought it meant, I simply asked him, "Do you ever feel sorry for yourself?" His reply was, "All the time."

There are many other fish, birds, mammals, reptiles, insects, and spiders named in the Bible—far too many to discuss individually. One more that we should discuss, though, is the spider. "The spider taketh hold with her hands, and is in kings' palaces" (Prov. 30:28).

Anyone who has ever tried ridding his house of spider webs has learned something about this little creature. "He takes hold with his hands," meaning, he's very tenacious. He *never* gives up. That's a very positive trait! On the other hand, what he builds with his hands is another story. I hate spider webs! Likewise, it would be hard to place a black widow spider into a positive setting. She's the epitome of evil.

Beavers are industrious; elephants are powerful; foxes are cunning; wolves run in packs and devour innocent lambs; lambs are defenseless; vipers are deadly; hogs are filthy; sharks are ruthless; mules are stubborn; monkeys are mischievous; fleas are insignificant; flies are unclean; sloths are lazy; snails are slow; moles are hidden; turkeys are dumb; swans are graceful; cats are predators; tigers are dangerous; giraffes are exalted; bears are grouchy; deer are swift; mice are timid; rats carry plagues; kangaroos jump; birds sing; goats butt; skunks stink; hornets sting; moths corrupt; rabbits increase; roaches infest; scorpions sting; dogs bite; the list goes on and on. Almost every creature has some characteristic that sets it apart and speaks clearly to those who have ears to hear. All we have to do is learn to listen.

Chapter Ten

Various Vehicles

A POPULAR TV SAFETY ADVERTISEMENT ends with a horrific car crash and advisedly says, "You can learn a lot from a dummy." No doubt that's true if you can find one that talks (especially after being decapitated in a crash)! Actually, you may not learn much from a dummy, but one thing you *can* learn from is your dreams, especially when you learn what the cars, trucks, vans, trains, and buses that you dream about are saying. When your ship comes in, it's carrying a message too, that is, if you're not waiting over at the airport.

Vehicles constantly appear in our dreams. They symbolize different things both to us and about us in the same way that our personal automobiles reveal a lot about ourselves. To illustrate, let's examine a few vehicles. The average person chooses a vehicle that suits his own personal tastes, that is, as far as his pocketbook will allow. The wealthy tycoon will choose an expensive sedan; the Don Juan, a sleek convertible; an exhibitionist, a sports car (or if he can't afford that, a jalopy with loud pipes). On the other hand, a house wife with several children wants a van, and a farmer, a tractor and a pickup truck. In each case, the vehicle is more than transportation; it's an extension of its owner.

Therefore, if God wants to talk to us about our family, He simply puts us into a van or SUV and off we go. If He wants to talk about our church family, He loads in a couple of children from other families in the church along with ours. Or He may just let the pastor drive. Of course, if the pastor's wife is driving, that's another story!

If He wants to warn us about trouble ahead, He may drive us down a muddy road. Or if the problem involves contention, there's another way of depicting it—the common fender bender. A dream about an automobile wreck may warn you of an impending clash with one of your peers. The carnage caused by "road rage" that we hear so much about is a natural expression of a spiritual problem. Through dreams, God can warn us about potential blowups (or blowouts, as the case may be), whether they happen in us or in one of our peers. Nahum may have been referring to something he saw in a dream when he prophesied of the high speed and hazardous transportation of our day: "The chariots shall rage in the streets, they shall justle one against another in the broad ways: they shall seem like torches, they shall run like the lightnings" (Nah. 2:4).

> One young lady dreamed that she was driving her husband's car at night. When she had car trouble, she stopped and looked in the trunk to discover a dead man. She was horrified, and ran and told her husband. He said, "Oh, don't worry; I'll take care of it." She realized that he was responsible for the presence of the dead man, and had no intention of reporting it to the authorities. She became fearful that she was going to get into trouble because of her involvement and was indecisive as to what she should do. Then she woke up.

The interpretation? Her husband was a cocaine addict. God was dealing with her about her codependence. She had to decide if she should leave and thus bring him into accountability for the error of his ways or not.

Crashes in the Ministry

BESIDES TALKING TO US about family and church matters, and warning us about trouble ahead, God also uses vehicles when He wants to talk to us about our ministry. Teachers usually dream about school buses, prophets about airplanes. Of course, prophet-teachers may dream about both at one time or another.

When I was very young in ministry, the pastor of the church I attended began to fall away from God. During that time, I had a dream:

> I was an aircraft mechanic at an airport. (In reality, I had earlier served as a jet mechanic in the US Air Force.) I was working on a helicopter and realized that it had a defective part. When I attempted to explain the problem to the pilot (who was the pastor), he said, "Oh, that's not what's wrong; it's just a little overheated." I realized that he was just too lazy to care. I knew he was wrong, but because he was in charge, I conceded and decided not to say anything more. Then I woke up.

A few weeks later, I dreamed:

> I was a passenger in a large airliner. I was conscious that there was very little food on board. I realized the plane was having engine trouble so I prayed and asked God if it was going to crash. He answered, "Yes, it will crash." I asked, "Will there be any survivors?" He said, "Eighteen will survive." After flying for a short time longer, the plane turned into a helicopter. Soon afterward, it turned into a blimp. Then the scene changed. Although I wasn't conscious of any crash, suddenly we were all in the ocean in chest-deep water. It was night, and there was no land in sight.

It wasn't long after I had these two dreams that things begin to "go sour" at church. Among other things, the pastor left with another man's wife. After the smoke cleared, the assistant pastor called a meeting to discuss the church's condition. Exactly eighteen "survivors" showed up for the meeting. I wasn't surprised, only disappointed. The defective condition and progressive changes in the airplane accurately depicted the deteriorating condition of the church during that time. The pastor was selfishly unconcerned, even though many people were hurt in the church's "crash."

In both of these dreams, the church was depicted as some type of airplane, and the pastor as the pilot. In the first dream, the helicopter represented the "hovering" condition of the church.

Although the church had taken off with great power and speed not long before, at the time of the dream, it was hovering stationary in the air. (For about six months prior to this dream, the church had been having a phenomenal revival both in spirit and numerical growth, but the revival had begun to wane.) The pilot was warned that the defective part had to be repaired, or the helicopter would certainly crash.

In the second dream, again the church was represented by an airplane. This time it was a fully loaded airliner. (The church had about one hundred members at that time.) As it flew it changed into a helicopter, but only hovered for a short time. Then it became a blimp. Unlike powered planes, blimps are moved by the winds. Likewise, this church began to be "tossed to and fro, and carried about with every wind of doctrine" (Eph. 4:14). I was warned and informed throughout this experience. Although I was not able to prevent the impending crash, I wasn't caught by surprise because God clearly showed me what was happening. I also received several dreams at that time showing me what to do, and what not to do, in regard to what was happening.

Years later, I experienced a similar dream, but this time it was about two ministers whom I knew, and their individual downfalls:

A short, powerful, jet fighter was taking off. I saw the plane's tail had been modified. It had a clamp on it that wasn't supposed to be there. The pilot began to do low-altitude stunts. At first, all went well; but then, he tightened the rolls (actually end-over-end cartwheels) and lost altitude. He hit the ground, bounced, and went straight up! At first, it looked like he had recovered, but then the jet blew up. Debris began to rain down. The fallout was going to be dangerous, especially if the engine was to fall on someone. A small nut hit me. I was dodging to stay out of the fallout. I went around the falling debris to avoid getting hit.

I saw the two pilots parachuting down and said, "Thank God they got out safe." I saw that someone on the ground was with the one who landed first. I waited for the second one to land. I told someone (an investigator?) that the pilot had been doing aerobatics at 1200 feet, and that he had failed to keep, or hold, a reference point; therefore, he crashed.

There is only one reference point that never changes—the Word of God. When this young minister lost sight of *the* reference that all things are judged by, and began to trust in his own understanding, he lost control and crashed. Much later, the other pilot also came drifting down, long after the fallout from the first one had settled.

Transportation in the Bible

YOU MAY BE WONDERING if anything like this is in the Bible. Although airplanes and automobiles were not yet invented when the Bible was written, horses, wagons, chariots, and even iron chariots were in daily use. Horses and ordinary chariots were used much as we use cars; and donkeys, mules, camels, and wagons were used like trucks. Iron chariots were the armored tanks of their day. There were no airplanes, but that didn't seem to bother God. When He wanted to take someone somewhere in a hurry, He just took him in His own private jet:

And when they were come up out of the water, the Spirit of the Lord caught away Philip, that the eunuch saw him no more.... But Philip was found at Azotus: and passing through he preached in all the cities, till he came to Caesarea (Acts 8:39-40).

How's that for first-class travel? Faster than the Concord! Philip didn't have to wait around at the airport for his luggage, either.

Ships and boats were common in Bible days, too. In fact, Paul used "shipwreck" as a metaphor for the modern, Laodicean church's "greasy grace" doctrine: "Holding faith, and a good conscience; which some having put away concerning faith have made shipwreck" (1 Tim. 1:19). In our society, the metaphor more likely used is "train wreck" or "plane crash."

James used the picture of a ship in a different way. He compared the ship's helm to a proud tongue:

Behold also the ships, which though they be so great, and are driven of fierce winds, yet are they turned about with a very small helm, whithersoever the governor listeth. Even so the tongue is a little member, and boasteth great things. Behold, how great a matter a little fire kindleth! (James 3:4-5)

It's not hard to turn a ship, but an unskilled skipper may capsize it if he tries turning it too fast. He also may run into rapids unless he knows how to steer clear of them.

The Travels of Jesus

A S HE SO OFTEN DID, Jesus gave us one of His living parables during His ministry at Lake Gennesaret:

And it came to pass, that, as the people pressed upon Him to hear the word of God, He stood by the lake of Gennesaret....And He entered into one of the ships, which was Simon's, and prayed him that he would thrust out a little from the land. And He sat down, and taught the people out of the ship (Luke 5:1,3).

After Peter received the Holy Spirit, Christ caused him to separate himself from "land" (carnal ways) and began to preach through him. Peter's ship represented Peter himself. Likewise, in the following Scripture, the disciples' ship represents their lives being tossed by a storm. But when Jesus stepped into their situation, their problems were over:

And when even was now come, His disciples went down unto the sea, and entered into a ship, and went over the sea toward Capernaum. And it was now dark, and Jesus was not come to them. And the sea arose by reason of a great wind that blew. So when they had rowed about five and twenty or thirty furlongs, they see Jesus walking on the sea, and drawing nigh unto the ship: and they were afraid. But He saith unto them, It is I; be not afraid. Then they willingly received Him into the ship: and immediately the ship was at the land whither they went (John 6:16-21).

And one more beautiful, living, ship parable right from the pages of Scripture occurs after Jesus had finished teaching the people. He commanded Peter to push off from shore, saying, "Launch out into the deep, and let down your nets."

Now when He had left speaking, He said unto Simon, Launch out into the deep, and let down your nets for a draught. And Simon answering said unto Him, Master, we have toiled all the night, and have taken nothing: nevertheless at Thy word I will let down the net. And when they had this done, they enclosed a great multitude of fishes: and their net brake. And they beckoned unto their partners, which were in the other ship, that they should come and help them. And they came, and filled both the ships, so that they began to sink (Luke 5:4-7).

Can't you just see the "catch" when revival comes? Instead of building a bigger church to hold the new converts, a church will invite their "partners" to come and receive the surplus into their churches. Hopefully, we'll soon reach that place of spiritual maturity and unselfishness before Jesus returns.

Other Types of Traffic

OTHER THAN CAMEL CARAVANS, there is nothing else similar to trains recorded in Scripture. However, they are rather common in dreams. They usually communicate one of two things: something *traditional*, since trains run on tracks and cannot easily change directions, or a *continuous* chain of events, since they are composed of a "chain" of cars. In fact, sometimes a simple iron chain can also mean "without interruption." When used as a pun, a *train* means "training," as in being taught. In addition, *railroad tracks* can have a dual meaning. The most common is "tradition" or "habit" because they're always the same, but a more subtle meaning is "caution." One should stop, look, and listen before crossing tracks because of the obvious danger. On the positive side, *trains* can refer to "staying on track," as in Paul's admonition to the Thessalonians: "Therefore, brethren, stand fast, and hold the traditions which ye have been taught, whether by word, or our epistle" (2 Thess. 2:15).

Military vehicles, such as tanks, fighter jets, bombers, battleships, and navy destroyers usually indicate spiritual warfare. Soldiers in uniform also fall into this category.

Large trucks, such as eighteen-wheelers, may represent large churches, or simply indicate large burdens and responsibilities. I once dreamed I was driving someone else's freight truck. Someone told me that in three years I would be given the title to it. At the time of the dream, I was assisting another minister, pastoring a small church. Three years later, I was called upon to be the senior pastor.

Pickup trucks usually refer to individual works and personal ministries. They can depict one's secular job or spiritual ministry. A pickup with a dead battery won't start. A truck with a flat tire won't roll. A minister without a fresh charge of God's Spirit won't do either. Sometimes we need to trade in our old pickup and get one with a more powerful engine. Of course, we'll have to pay the price, but that can't be helped.

Specialty vehicles have a lot to say, too. An ambulance comes to our aid, but I'd just as soon not need one. A school bus takes us to school when we need to learn something new. A bulldozer overcomes everything in its path and can make a way where there is no way. A farm tractor plows and plants, and a combine harvests that which was sown. There's a message in each and every one of these if we're listening to what they have to say.

The King's Highway

IF WE DREAM OF DRIVING BACKWARD, looking over our shoulder, we're going by our past experiences instead of being led by the Spirit. If we drive backward by looking in the rearview mirrors, we are ministering by the letter of the Word instead of by the inspiration of the Spirit. Paul said that God "hath made us able ministers of the new testament; not of the letter, but of the spirit: for the letter killeth, but the spirit giveth life" (2 Cor. 3:6). We must drive forward, facing forward, to pass God's driver's exam.

An old gravel road often represents God's highway: "Thus saith the Lord, Stand ye in the ways, and see, and ask for the old paths, where is the good way, and walk therein, and ye shall find rest for your souls. But they said, We will not walk therein" (Jer. 6:16).

Why a gravel road? The rocks represent God's Word. But even a wooded path through the forest can be His way too. "Thy word is a lamp unto my feet, and a light unto my path" (Ps. 119:105). And in rare cases, even the *freeway* can be the right way. But getting in the fast lane on the *expressway* is usually not His way:

> *Enter ye in at the strait gate: for wide is the gate, and broad is the way, that leadeth to destruction, and many there be which go in thereat* (Matthew 7:13).

Sometimes we are inconvenienced by having to take a detour. Other times we might find ourselves on a dead-end street. A muddy road indicates fleshy desires and temptations. A rocky road speaks for itself. Paved roads are better, smoother, and usually mean that God has us on the right road to get us where He wants us to go, that is, if we heed the signs like we're supposed to. Maps help too, and there's no map more accurate than the Word of God.

Train stations, bus stations, and airports all mean the same—waiting. And waiting is something that no one enjoys. Waiting to depart indicates waiting on God's timing before embarking on some venture that He has assigned us to. Waiting for someone's arrival may indicate you're anticipating a divine appointment (whether you are aware of it or not). Whether we're waiting or traveling down the King's highway, driving or riding as a passenger, it all has meaning. Whatever means of transportation we find ourselves using, whatever circumstances we find ourselves in, all situations speak volumes if we're listening. Come to think of it, you *can* learn a lot from a dummy.

Chapter Eleven

That's All, Folks!

WELL, *ELEVEN* MEANS "END," and this is the eleventh chapter, so I'll have to wind it up. But before closing, I want to cover several categories that don't contain enough items to each warrant a separate chapter, yet they're too important to ignore. They include the metals that we haven't already discussed. One verse of Scripture names almost every one of them: "Only the gold, and the silver, the brass, the iron, the tin, and the lead" (Num. 31:22).

Metals Other Than Silver and Gold

WE'VE ALREADY DISCUSSED *gold* and *silver* in Chapter Seven about colors. Remember, *gold* is "glory" and "wisdom," and *silver* represents "knowledge," including intimate knowledge. Now we'll examine brass, iron, tin, and lead. Also, Ezra mentioned copper, and Paul referred to a coppersmith named Alexander.

It's easy to glean the meaning for *iron* from Scripture. It means "strength." Sometimes the Bible refers to an "iron yoke of bondage"; other times it compares iron to the strength of God's Spirit given to break heavy yokes off of its victims. Either way, "strength" is the primary meaning. Joshua told Israel they would, "drive out the Canaanites, though they have *iron* chariots, and *though they be strong*" (Josh. 17:18, emphasis added). He knew they could do all things through Christ who strengthened them (see Phil. 4:13).

Tin usually means "cheap," "weak," even "worthless." "And I will turn my hand upon thee, and purely purge away thy dross, and take away all thy tin" (Is. 1:25). Tin is just not worth much, and lead is not much better. It's heavy, and often represents heavy burdens, grievous to be borne. "And, behold, there was lifted up a talent of lead: and this is a woman that sitteth in the midst of the ephah. And he said, This is wickedness. And he cast it into the midst of the ephah; and he cast the weight of lead upon the mouth thereof" (Zech. 5:7-8). Well, that's one way to get rid of witchcraft!

Copper and brass are related, because ancient brass is an alloy of copper and tin. In Bible days, pure copper was considered as valuable as gold: "Also twenty basins of gold...and two vessels of fine copper, precious as gold" (Ezra 8:27). Both, in one way or another, represent words—sometimes God's Word, sometimes man's. Probably the most famous occurrence of brass in Scripture is John's description of Jesus whom he witnessed while he was on the isle of Patmos:

> *And in the midst of the seven candlesticks one like unto the Son of man, clothed with a garment down to the foot, and girt about the paps with a golden girdle. His head and His hairs were white like wool, as white as snow; and His eyes were as a flame of fire; and His **feet like unto fine brass**, as if they burned in a furnace; and His voice as the sound of many waters* (Revelation 1:13-15, emphasis added).

In the natural, we walk with our feet. In the spirit, we walk with our words. Jesus' feet being as fine brass depicts the pure Word of God: "The words of the Lord are pure words: as silver tried in a furnace of earth, purified seven times" (Ps. 12:6).

Here His Word is declared to be completely pure. In fact, it is purified the same way silver is purified—by fire. *Fire* and *affliction* are synonymous: "Behold, I have refined thee, but not with silver; I have chosen thee in the furnace of affliction" (Is. 48:10). Jesus didn't just preach the Word, He *was* the Word. He was purified in the furnace of affliction and came forth as fine brass.

God's Gold or Man's Brass

As with most other symbols, the meaning for *brass* can be reversed, too. *Brass* can mean the cheap, impure word of man. Several times in Scripture we find hallowed, gold shields being replaced with brass ones. Boy, that speaks volumes! It usually happened after God left and went someplace where He felt more welcome. Without Him around, Israel was easy pickings for their warlike neighbors. So they usually tried to bribe their way out of bad situations by giving God's gold away. Then, the place looked kind of empty, so they replaced it with brass. Anyway, gold and brass look a lot alike if you keep the brass polished; so who cares?

> *And it came to pass in the fifth year of king Rehoboam, that Shishak king of Egypt came up against Jerusalem...and he took away all the **shields of gold** which Solomon had made. And king Rehoboam made in their stead **brazen shields**, and committed them unto the hands of the chief of the guard...* (1 Kings 14:25-27, emphasis added).

This discussion may be a little more serious than first meets the eye. God's gold is God's glory. Our shield is God's glory, not His promises. His promises are conditional. We seldom live up to them. His glory is the reason He gives us grace and keeps the devil off our necks when we can't meet His conditions. Whenever we lose faith, or He gets disgusted enough to turn us over to our enemies, whichever comes first, we're in a heap of trouble. But thank God, it takes a lot to get Him disgusted. That's why our shield depends upon the measure of faith we're able to acquire. Let's take a look at a couple of Scriptures:

> *And the Lord said unto Moses, I have seen this people, and, behold, it is a stiffnecked people: now therefore let Me alone, that My wrath may wax hot against them, and that I may consume them: and I will make of thee a great nation. And Moses besought the Lord his God, and said, Lord, why doth Thy wrath wax hot against Thy people, which Thou hast brought forth out of the land of Egypt with great power, and with a mighty hand? **Wherefore should the Egyptians speak, and say, For mischief did He bring them out, to slay them in the mountains, and to consume them from the face of the earth?** Turn from Thy fierce wrath, and repent of this evil against Thy people. Remember Abraham, Isaac, and Israel, Thy servants, **to whom Thou**

swarest by Thine own self, and *saidst unto them, I will multi-*
ply your seed as the stars of heaven, and all this land that I
have spoken of will I give unto your seed, and they shall inher-
it it for ever. And the Lord repented of the evil which He
thought to do unto His people (Exodus 32:9-14, emphasis
added).

Take note that Moses pointed out that if God didn't do what
He had promised, even though Israel failed to meet His conditions, He was going to lose face. The Egyptians simply wouldn't
understand. They would only see that the Israelites' God had
failed to perform what He had promised! Moses correctly saw that
God would lose face regardless of whose fault it was. So often it's
that way, and God knows it. Therefore, His stated policy is:

For Mine own sake, even for Mine own sake, will I do it: for
how should My name be polluted? and I will not give My glory
unto another (Isaiah 48:11).

So when we replace His glory with ours, replacing gold with
brass, sooner or later we fail. Brass shields just won't do. God will
not defend your reputation. He'll only defend His! If you take His
glory, you're on your own. So, "Above all, taking the shield of
faith, wherewith ye shall be able to quench all the fiery darts of the
wicked" (Eph. 6:16).

If you trust in your own righteousness, declaring to God how
you've met all His conditions, which no man can truly meet, you've
deceived yourself. You're holding up a brass shield against an
enemy who cannot be defeated without God's intervention. Only
one warrior has ever successfully bruised satan's head. And He'll
do it again when we trust in Him: "And the God of peace shall
bruise satan under your feet shortly. The grace of our Lord Jesus
Christ be with you" (Rom. 16:20). Notice it's "the God of peace"
who bruises satan, not the person God is using to accomplish it.

Now why did we discuss all that? We are supposed to be discussing dream symbols, not theology! Oh, but we are. Take note of
all that we've covered. *Fire* often depicts trials and afflictions. *Brass*
represents either God's Word, or ours. *Gold shields* portray God's
glory and *brass shields*, man's substitutes. And above all, different

metals can tell the whole story once we have the fundamental understanding of how they are used.

A Person's Name and Trade

N OW, WHY DO YOU THINK that Paul went to the trouble of telling us that Alexander the troublemaker was a coppersmith? We can only guess, but we can make an educated guess. Let's examine that passage of Scripture:

> *Alexander the coppersmith did me much evil: the Lord reward him according to his works: of whom be thou ware also; for he hath greatly withstood our words. **At my first answer** no man stood with me, but all men forsook me: I pray God that it may not be laid to their charge* (2 Timothy 4:14-16, emphasis added).

Alexander was one of Paul's accusers; we can be almost certain of that. Otherwise, Paul wouldn't have been "answering" him. But Alexander wasn't just another Jew accusing Paul of preaching against Moses' Law. To begin with, the name "Alexander" is Greek, not Hebrew. Alexander was probably a philosopher. Why a philosopher? Because he was a coppersmith. Have you ever noticed how often God uses a person's name to describe his character, and his trade to tell us something about his ministry? (For instance, look at what Peter and John were doing when Jesus first called them—Matthew 4:18,21.) *Alexander* means "man-defender," and he used copper to fabricate things. I believe Alexander had more flaws in his gnostic doctrines than dents in his pots and pans. Only someone who could fabricate doctrines deceitful enough to sway others away from the simple truth of the gospel would prompt such a warning from Paul:

> *Beware lest any man spoil you through philosophy and vain deceit, after the tradition of men, after the rudiments of the world, and not after Christ* (Colossians 2:8).

Oh, well, it's only a theory. We won't know for sure one way or the other until we ask Paul in person, and that may not be as long as some may think!

Power and Authority

A LEXANDER THE TROUBLEMAKER brings us to another subject— people. People identify themselves in different ways, and often their identity gives special meaning to their appearances in dreams. For example, almost everyone has dreamed about police. These men and women are the epitome of authority. Sometimes their authority is used properly, to protect us; sometimes they abuse their authority and use it selfishly. Either way, *power and authority* is the primary meaning, and *protection* and *abuse* are branches of the same. Subsequently, policemen may be for or against us. They may represent God's angels or satan's demons. They can even represent themselves, if we actually know them in person.

When soldiers appear in dreams, they represent force and power, similar to police. The might of the armed forces may represent the hosts of the armies of the Lord, and a general may represent Christ Himself. A foreign army usually stands for satan's forces.

Doctors are similar because they're also licensed authorities; however, their real authority comes from their *knowledge*, not from government. They usually imply healing in one form or another. Sometimes a good doctor represents the Great Physician. In the same way, college professors and lawyers are authorities by reason of their knowledge.

Besides power that comes through military might and physical strength, and the influence that comes through knowledge, there are two other divisions of authority that can be closely related to one another: political power, which is influence and authority obtained by *position*; and wealth. A rich man's power and influence is by reason of his vast *resources*. Often, power hungry people are seldom satisfied with the limited power they have, so they attempt to broaden their influence into other areas as well. Wealthy men run for political office; lawyers become senators; and poor politicians use their influence to obtain wealth.

If God wants to talk to us about our strength or weakness, our power, or lack thereof, He may use someone in one of these four divisions of authority to illustrate His message. There are four areas of spiritual authority and power that closely parallel these four natural divisions. It helps to understand the comparisons.

Man's military might is no match for God's mighty power; however, His power and might are often represented by man's machinery and weapons. Jesus said, "But ye shall receive power, after that the Holy Ghost is come upon you" (Acts 1:8a). The "power" promised here is the Greek word *dunamis*. It means "force." In fact, it's usually translated, "miracle."

The power and influence obtained through education also has a spiritual parallel: "A wise man is strong; yea, a man of knowledge increaseth strength" (Prov. 24:5). The difference as to whether his strength is carnal or spiritual depends upon what type of knowledge he has. Paul said:

> *...I count all things but loss for the excellency of the knowledge of Christ Jesus my Lord: for whom I have suffered the loss of all things, and do count them but dung, that I may win Christ....That I may know Him, and the power of His resurrection...* (Philippians 3:8,10).

Godly spiritual power and authority obtained through knowledge can only come from personal, intimate knowledge of God.

Political power is influence and authority obtained through position. The spiritual authority that parallels political authority is probably the most abused and misused power in the church:

> *But Jesus called them unto Him, and said, Ye know that the princes of the Gentiles exercise dominion over them, and they that are great exercise authority upon them. But it shall not be so among you: but whosoever will be great among you, let him be your minister; and whosoever will be chief among you, let him be your servant* (Matthew 20:25-27).

The full implication of this passage of Scripture is beyond the scope of this book, but the correlation between politicians and pastors, elders, apostles, etc. should be obvious enough for everyone to see how God may use one to represent the other.

Governors and presidents usually represent Christ, unless they're crooked (in the dream, not in real life). The president's true character seldom enters into the picture—only his position. Otherwise, God couldn't use any of them to represent Himself. Even "Honest Abe" wasn't that pure.

The fourth division, power obtained through wealth, also has its spiritual parallel. Solomon compared wealth to the knowledge of God, and concluded that the knowledge of God is far greater in value:

> *For wisdom is a defence, and money is a defence: but the excellency of knowledge is, that wisdom giveth life to them that have it* (Ecclesiastes 7:12).

Eternal life comes through unwavering faith in Jesus Christ alone. You can't buy it. When we know Him (not just know about Him), we have the *"riches of the full assurance of understanding..."* (Col. 2:2b, emphasis added). Full assurance is faith. *Faith is the currency of the Kingdom of God.* Abraham was prosperous because he was "strong in faith"; we should be too (see Rom. 4:20).

When God wants to point out something in any one of these four divisions of authority, He has an endless list of trades to choose from. The natural and social power and authority wielded by police, doctors, lawyers, politicians, business men, oil tycoons, and others closely parallels the spiritual power of godly men in the Kingdom of God: "But when the multitudes saw it, they marvelled, and glorified God, which had given such power unto men" (Mt. 9:8).

God Uses All People

BESIDES AUTHORITY, there are several other things that tradesmen can depict. Telephone repairmen, automobile mechanics, crooks, thieves—there is no limit to the number of people that God can use when He needs to talk to us. A telephone repairman may show up to inform us that God is getting a busy signal every time He tries to call, or a car mechanic may tell us that we need a Holy Ghost oil change in our life.

At other times, relationships tell the story. Mothers are our source; fathers are our authority. In-laws are occasionally out-laws, depending upon whether we have a good relationship with them or not. Sometimes, the word *law* is the clue we need to get the message. It was Moses' father-in-law that advised him how to set up elders to keep order in the camp (see Ex. 18:12-23). Elders should still enforce the ordinances established by each local church. On the other hand, if they act legalistically, they may attempt to enforce laws that the members aren't really obliged to keep.

The pastor may portray Christ in a dream, because he represents Him when he speaks before the church. Subsequently, his wife may typify the church. Our natural father may represent our heavenly Father, and our natural mother, our church. A woman's husband may stand for Christ because, "he [or she] that is joined unto the Lord is one spirit" (1 Cor. 6:17), or he can portray the devil, depending upon the character of the husband! An ex-husband may represent a Christian woman's relationship with the world before she "married" Christ.

Brothers and sisters, as well as old friends and acquaintances, often portray ourselves. One of the neatest tricks that dreams play on us is to incorporate several different people in one dream and have everyone of them correspond to a different aspect of ourselves. It's very common to dream of three different people—one for the spirit, one for the soul, and one for the body—all in the same dream. Sounds like *me, myself,* and *I;* doesn't it? Evil sometimes comes in threes, too.

At times, our children represent ourselves, and sometimes themselves. They can even stand for those in our church, especially if there are church children with them in the dream.

And last, but not least, grandparents usually depict the past. Whether a person is dead or alive doesn't always enter into the picture. In God's eyes, they're all still alive. Actually, the dream usually refers to what we have inherited from them:

When I call to remembrance the unfeigned faith that is in thee, which dwelt first in thy grandmother Lois, and thy mother Eunice; and I am persuaded that in thee also (2 Timothy 1:5).

It should be obvious that if we can inherit our grandmother's faith, we can also inherit her faults. If God wants to point out either of these, why wouldn't He just put her into our dreams? As we discussed in the chapter on directions, you may appear in her house, or you may dream of her dress or jewelry. Of course, this applies to grandpa's stuff, too.

Acts of God

ANOTHER GROUP OF RELATED SYMBOLS that are very common in dreams are acts of God. Even though most good things that happen are also acts of God, I'm referring to the insurance companies' definition. They blame things like fire, storms, earthquakes, and volcanoes on Him. They reason that if the world self-destructs, it is His fault because He created it. They blame everything that destroys property and hurts people without their help on Him. It could be that they're right.

Fires, tornadoes, floods, and other natural disasters usually come in two different categories: good and bad. You might be wondering how a violent storm could be considered good; so let's take a quick look. Because God's power is so awesome, He often depicts His arrival as a storm. In fact, when He came down to Mount Sinai, He gave the Israelites a taste of all four—fire, storm, earthquake and volcano:

> *And it came to pass on the third day in the morning, that there were thunders and lightnings, and a thick cloud upon the mount, and the voice of the trumpet exceeding loud; so that all the people that was in the camp trembled....And mount Sinai was altogether on a smoke, because the Lord descended upon it in fire: and the smoke thereof ascended as the smoke of a furnace, and the whole mount quaked greatly* (Exodus 19:16,18).

Some people think that if a dream scares them, it's not from God. That's foolishness. When God sends His power, it usually scares the daylights out of our flesh, regardless of how spiritual we are. The Bible says God's arrival on Mount Sinai even scared Moses: "And so terrible was the sight, that Moses said, I exceedingly fear and quake" (Heb. 12:21). Thus, fear is not a proper yardstick to judge whether a dream is from God or not. If Noah had thought that way, he probably would have drowned:

> *By faith Noah, being warned of God of things not seen as yet, **moved with fear,** prepared an ark to the saving of his house; by the which he condemned the world, and became heir of the righteousness which is by faith* (Hebrews 11:7, emphasis added).

Joel seemed to be referring to atomic power when he prophesied of the endtime outpouring of the Holy Spirit: "And I will show wonders in the heavens and in the earth, blood, and fire, and pillars of smoke" (Joel 2:30). Sounds like a pretty good description of an atomic bomb explosion, especially for someone who hasn't seen one; wouldn't you say?

Atomic explosions, fires, storms, earthquakes, volcanos, even avalanches may signify a mighty move of God—storms and earthquakes in particular. Storms bring rain and lightning, and lightning is a type of power from Heaven. Earthquakes often signify repentance. Our flesh is made of earth, so when we quake like Moses, we're repenting.

Volcanoes are also acts of God, but we can have our own little volcanic eruption without God's help. Sometimes when we explode in anger, we erupt like a miniature volcano. But according to James, "The wrath of man worketh not the righteousness of God" (Jas. 1:20), so we can't blame our rage on God. On the other hand, if someone is mad at us, God may let us know about it by also portraying it as a fiery volcano.

Sometimes before earthquakes and volcanoes appear, they are preceded with earth tremors. Likewise, sometimes before we erupt, we are given some advance warnings, if we're listening. God can prevent "volcanoes" from erupting and keep "earthquakes" from tearing down everything we've built, *if* we're paying attention. Similarly, He can warn us when a tornado or hurricane is coming so that we can take preventive measures, whether the storm is literal or in the spiritual realm.

Raging fires may depict any number of things, including revival, destruction, or passion. It pays to seek God for the specific meaning when we dream of potentially destructive "acts" like these. Paul used *burn* as a metaphor for inordinate lust:

> *And likewise also the men, leaving the natural use of the woman,* **burned in their lust** *one toward another; men with men working that which is unseemly, and receiving in themselves that recompence of their error which was meet* (Romans 1:27, emphasis added).

One's automobile usually represents one's life. Consequently, if your car is on fire, it may mean you're being consumed by passion. What kind of passion? God used fire to describe His own burning anger: "For a fire is kindled in Mine anger, and shall burn unto the lowest hell, and shall consume the earth with her increase, and set on fire the foundations of the mountains" (Deut. 32:22). Anger, hatred, and lust are all portrayed by fire.

Fires, like most other symbols, can be positive too. Not all fire is destructive. In fact, some fire can be quite instructive!

And the angel of the Lord appeared unto [Moses] in a flame of fire out of the midst of a bush: and he looked, and, behold, the bush burned with fire, and the bush was not consumed....And when the Lord saw that he turned aside to see, God called unto him out of the midst of the bush, and said, Moses, Moses. And he said, Here am I (Exodus 3:2,4).

When Moses turned aside to see what the fire was all about, the angel of the Lord spoke to him and set his heart ablaze. He fanned the passion back into flame that Moses once had for his brethren. Zeal for God's children is a good passion to have.

The Four Seasons

THE FOUR SEASONS are another group of symbols that frequently serve as messengers in dreams. Spring speaks of revival and renewal. During this season, dead things suddenly spring into life. It is a time of refreshing after the long, dreary winter. It may foretell of a "new thing" that God is causing to "spring forth" in the land: "Behold, I will do a new thing; now it shall spring forth; shall ye not know it? I will even make a way in the wilderness, and rivers in the desert" (Is. 43:19).

Summer, on the other hand, is a time of toil and labor: "He that gathereth in summer is a wise son: but he that sleepeth in harvest is a son that causeth shame" (Prov. 10:5). It may also represent trials because of the intense heat and droughts that many parts of the country endure during this time.

Autumn is colorful, beautiful, and implies that summer is over. Times are changing. Old things pass away to make room for new. Sometimes these changes are for the better; sometimes for the worse: "The harvest is past, the summer is ended, and we are not saved" (Jer. 8:20). Sometimes the changes refer to putting off our old traditions to make room for new ways to come as when a tree drops its leaves in preparation of forming new buds for spring.

The winter season usually implies waiting. It is a time of planning and preparation for spring planting. Sometimes it portrays a period of desolation and barrenness in one's life. The coldness of winter may speak of rejection and isolation. The four seasons are summed up in God's promise of their perpetuity:

While the earth remaineth, seedtime and harvest, and cold and heat, and summer and winter, and day and night shall not cease (Genesis 8:22).

Rain and snow are closely associated with the cycle of nature. A winter setting with a snow-covered hillside may reveal God's continual mercy upon the land. The snow represents His righteous covering and winter a period of patient waiting upon God. A soaking rain may represent His Spirit being poured out upon a dry and thirsty land. It can also portray the misery of being without shelter in a time of trouble. In the Bible, Isaiah used clouds, rain, and snow as metaphors for both our thoughts and God's, and for God's Word:

*For My thoughts are not your thoughts, neither are your ways My ways, saith the Lord. For as the heavens are higher than the earth, so are My ways higher than your ways, and My thoughts than your thoughts. For as the **rain** cometh down, **and the snow from heaven**, and returneth not thither, but watereth the earth, and maketh it bring forth and bud, that it may give seed to the sower, and bread to the eater: so shall My word be that goeth forth out of My mouth: it shall not return unto Me void, but it shall accomplish that which I please, and it shall prosper in the thing whereto I sent it* (Isaiah 55:8-11, emphasis added).

The Lights of the Heavens

THERE'S ONE MORE GROUP of symbols that everyone should be familiar with: the sun, the stars, and the moon. If one doesn't understand the spiritual significance of these three symbols, many Scriptures remain a mystery. Likewise, when they appear in our dreams, their message remains a mystery, too. All three of these were made on the fourth day of creation. Earlier we saw that *four* means "rule." Let's take a closer look at what God made on the fourth day:

*And God said, Let there be lights in the firmament of the heaven to divide the day from the night; and let them be for signs, and for seasons, and for days, and years: and let them be for lights in the firmament of the heaven to give light upon the earth: and it was so. And God made two great lights; the **greater light** to rule the day, and the **lesser light** to rule the night: He made the **stars** also* (Genesis 1:14-16, emphasis added).

The greater light no doubt refers to the sun. It doesn't take much research to learn that God made this light to represent Himself: "For the Lord God is a *sun* and shield..." (Ps. 84:11, emphasis added). And notice God's pun in the following verse: "But unto you that fear My name shall the *Sun* of righteousness arise with healing in His wings" (Mal. 4:2a, emphasis added).

The stars are relatively easy to understand too: "And they that be wise shall shine as the brightness of the firmament; and they that turn many to righteousness as the stars for ever and ever" (Dan. 12:3). In fact, both the sun and stars, plus the moon, were used in one of two dreams that got Joseph into so much trouble:

> *And he dreamed yet another dream, and told it his brethren, and said, Behold, I have dreamed a dream more; and, behold, the **sun** and the **moon** and the eleven **stars** made obeisance to me. And he told it to his father [Jacob], and to his brethren: and his father rebuked him, and said unto him, What is this dream that thou hast dreamed? Shall I and thy mother and thy brethren indeed come to bow down ourselves to thee to the earth?* (Genesis 37:9-10, emphasis added).

Jacob understood the symbolism of his son's dream all too well. He just didn't like what it meant. Jacob was Joseph's father, and he knew the sun represented himself. God is our heavenly Father, and God said the sun represented Him and His Son. So we see that the sun can represent our *father*, either heavenly or earthly, and it can also represent Christ. Jacob realized the eleven stars represented Joseph's brothers, and Daniel said stars represent Christ's witnesses. Either way, they represent people. Also, Jacob referred to the moon as Joseph's mother. Joseph was a type of Jesus, and his mother represented the Church. Jesus said, "My mother and My brethren are these which hear the word of God, and do it" (Lk. 8:21b). Those who hear the Word and practice it are believers. Collectively, the believers are the Body of Christ, which is the Church.

Stars represent each of God's children individually, and the moon represents God's children collectively. "And [God] hath raised us up together, and made us sit together in heavenly places in Christ Jesus" (Eph. 2:6). The Church is "the *lesser light*" that God set in the heavens "to rule the night." We receive the light of the "Son" and reflect it to a world that lies in darkness. All sinners are in darkness: "For they that sleep sleep in the night; and they that be drunken are drunken in the night" (1 Thess. 5:7).

In summary, the sun represents God; the stars depict the saints; and the moon portrays the Church. What is the significance of all this? To answer that, we'll first examine a very important end-time Scripture and then we'll look at a prophetic dream that God gave me several years ago. When God promised that He would give us dreams, He also made a reference to the sun and moon:

> *And it shall come to pass **in the last days**, saith God, I will pour out of My Spirit upon all flesh: and your sons and your daughters shall prophesy, and your young men shall see visions, and your old men **shall dream dreams**....The **sun** shall be turned into darkness, and the **moon** into blood, before that great and notable day of the Lord come* (Acts 2:17,20, emphasis added).

This Scripture has nothing to do with the natural sun or moon. The early Church suffered severe persecution. The latter Church will too. "The lesser light" that God made "to rule the night" will be turned into blood. "The greater light" that He made "to rule the day" won't be giving much light at that time either. To further clarify this analysis, take a close look at the following Scripture:

> *Moreover the light of the moon shall be as the light of the sun, and the light of the sun shall be sevenfold, as the light of seven days, in the day that the Lord bindeth up the breach of Hs people, and healeth the stroke of their wound* (Isaiah 30:26).

If the natural sun's light ever gets seven times brighter, it will also get seven times hotter. Talk about a barbecue! If that happens, we won't be here for Jesus to come back for. *Sevenfold* simply means a complete unfolding. Before Jesus returns, God is going to give the Church the full revelation of Himself. Therefore the Church's light will be "as the light of the *Son*" (pun intended). At that time Jesus' promise will be fulfilled where He said, "Verily, verily, I say unto you, He that believeth on Me, the works that I do shall he do also; and greater works than these shall he do; because I go unto My Father" (Jn. 14:12). Now let's take a look at my dream:

> On December 6, 1985, I dreamed about the moon. It was a bright, beautiful, full moon. It was being approached by

a large mass of earthen material that was traveling through space. It was as though a planet had been crushed and the loose debris was going to collide with the moon. The crushed material was divided into two waves of tan-colored dirt. The total mass of the waves was so great that if both were to hit the moon at once, I knew the moon would be knocked completely out of orbit! Therefore, the mass was divided into two waves, the second larger than the first. I realized the moon would be greatly enlarged as a result of each impact. Then I awoke.

I wrote the interpretation in my dream journal. The moon is the Church (which sits in heavenly places with Christ). The large mass of earthen material is people from every nation being drawn toward the Church. (The tan color shows that these people are dead in trespasses and sins.) The two waves are two approaching revivals. If God saves everyone that He plans on saving all at one time, the Church will not be able to absorb the increase (it will be knocked out of orbit); therefore, He has divided the endtime harvest into two consecutive waves. The second wave of revival is going to be larger than the first. (*Since I had this dream, the first wave of revival has already begun in many parts of the world.*)

The only symbol in this dream that we haven't discussed is the *dirt*. The Bible says our bodies are made of dust: "And the Lord God formed man of the dust of the ground, and breathed into his nostrils the breath of life; and man became a living soul" (Gen. 2:7). People are made of earth, so *earth* represents people. You can see why I interpreted the *tan* earth as sinners.

There are many more groups and divisions besides numbers, colors, animals, vehicles, metals, people, power, acts of God, the four seasons, and heavenly and earthly bodies to consider. These simply serve to illustrate the way a family of objects or actions are used to portray a complete picture. Each individual member adds to and complements the other members of its family. When you dream of something that belongs to a group not referred to in this book, simply meditate upon how it relates to the other members. By comparing it with its aunts and uncles, brothers and sisters, you can unearth "the rest of the story."

Chapter Twelve

Well, Almost All...

Y OU DIDN'T REALLY THINK that a preacher would actually conclude on his first closing, did you? Well, then you're not disappointed! There are some important rules to follow when interpreting dreams. You'll find some, but not all of these rules, along with a dictionary of symbols, in my first book, *Understanding the Dreams You Dream*, which complements this book.

Rules to Follow

T HE FIRST RULE: *Most dreams are messages to the dreamer, for the dreamer, about the dreamer.* This is probably the most important rule of all because it will save you from making major mistakes when interpreting dreams. When other people are in your dream, remember they are probably there to help you learn something about yourself, not to show you something about themselves. Of course, there are exceptions; but think of Paul's admonition before you decide that your dream is an exception to the rule: "And having in a readiness to revenge all disobedience, when your obedience is fulfilled" (2 Cor. 10:6).

The second rule: *You seldom know for sure that your interpretation is correct until you can apply it to a real-life situation.* This is what makes prophetic dreams so difficult to understand. Take the Book of Revelation, for example. Many people speculate what various prophetic Scriptures represent, but no one can be positive of his/her interpretation, except for those texts that have already come to pass and have become history. The parts that are still prophecy remain a mystery. Likewise, as long as the stage hasn't been set in your real life for the play that you've seen in your dream, you'll speculate about it too. (The primary exception to this rule is when God reveals the meaning.)

The dreamer's circumstances provide very important clues for interpreting dreams, because a dream may have a literal meaning. Without the proper application, it's impossible to know the correct interpretation. Here's a good example:

> A Christian lady dreamed that her teenage son was sick. When the doctor examined him, he said the lad needed more vitamin C. After her son became even worse, the mother returned him to the doctor. The doctor said, "I don't understand this. He just needs vitamin C, and it's real easy to get."

Because this dream could easily have a natural application, it would be unwise to attempt an interpretation without first asking the mother if her son was actually sick or not. If he was, by all means, she should get him some vitamin C! But if he wasn't (and in this case he wasn't), vitamin C wouldn't do him much good. It was simply a symbol for Christ. God was telling her that her boy, who had a problem with anger and rebellion, needed counseling.

Once you have determined the proper application for your dream, it's usually rather easy to interpret. Therefore, always try to discover what your dream applies to before trying to decide what it means. If you do that, you'll maintain a lot higher batting average than you would otherwise. How do you do that? Two additional rules will answer that question.

The third rule: *Most dreams are parables, and most objects that appear in dreams are symbols, including people.* Do not consider objects or people to be literal, unless it's obvious they are literal (and it usually is evident when they are).

The fourth rule relates to helping others interpret their dreams. When you get involved in dream interpretation and master a few fundamentals, your friends will soon find out and *presto*, you're an expert! When they see how good you are, invariably they'll start asking you for help. So to help you help them, here are a few guidelines that I've developed over the years.

This rule is very important: *It's always the dreamer's place to determine if the interpretation is right or wrong.* The best way to avoid breaking this rule is try *not* to interpret their dreams. Instead, ask them a few questions that will lead them to their own interpretations. Subsequently, they'll not only have more confidence in dreams and their meanings, but they'll also begin to understand how to interpret dreams for themselves. In fact, you can help yourself interpret your own dreams by asking yourself the same questions that you ask your friends. The order of these questions isn't critical, but it is logical:

1. What is the dream's subject? What is it about? What is the action? What are the people saying and doing? For instance, is there a storm coming? An opportunity? Remember, most dreams apply to the dreamer's present circumstances.

2. What past or present circumstances could the dream be applicable to? What situation in the dreamer's life could it address? What question has he or she recently asked? What problem is the dreamer facing? Is there internal conflict? Inhibitions? Insecurities? Anxieties? Are there decisions to be made? Directions to be obtained?

3. Who does the dream refer to (personal, church, family)? Who is in the dream? If there is a person in the dream other than the dreamer, what is his or her relationship to the dreamer, and what is the name, age, race, occupation, hobby, likes and dislikes of this person? If he or she is a stranger, who or what does this person remind the dreamer of?

4. Where is the setting located? In the dreamer's house? At the office? In a stranger's home?

5. When is the dream referring to (past, present, future)? Is someone of a different age in the dream than they presently are in reality? Is something from the past considered to be present?

6. Why was the dream given? What action is required? Repentance? Intercession? Is it a confirmation? Instruction? Warning?

7. What symbols are used? Besides the obvious, what emotions, thoughts, questions, or impressions did the dreamer experience while dreaming? To understand each individual symbol, ask the dreamer, "What does this symbol mean to YOU?" Use association.

Ask what the object, shape, number, color, vehicle, insect, animal, place, occupation, person, or name reminds them of?

8. And last, to summarize your investigation, ask the dreamer these three questions: What do *you* think the dream means? Who do you think it applies to? Why do you think you had the dream? And be gracious. It's always the dreamer's place to judge if the interpretation is right. Never force your interpretation upon anyone. "Therefore all things whatsoever ye would that men should do to you, do ye even so to them..." (Mt. 7:12).

Seek God's Help

BESIDES THE QUESTIONS posed above, ask God to give you *His* understanding of the dream. Joseph said interpretations belong to God. Apply the questions given above. Because many dreams are direct personal communication from God, He will often use symbols that mean something specific to the dreamer; therefore, a given symbol may not mean the same to someone else. For this reason, proper interpretation often requires insight from the one who actually dreamed the dream. Before venturing any interpretation concerning a specific symbol, remember to always ask the dreamer the question given above: "What does this object, color, person, etc. mean to YOU?" If using association does not provide any meaning to the dreamer (if it does not remind them of something or someone in particular), then use the universal meaning for the symbol to help determine what God is saying. Often the symbol's meaning may be obtained from the way it, or a similar symbol, is used in the Bible.

Even with all the information you've gathered, you still might not fully understand the dream. So, to arrive at the interpretation, dissect the dream into small parts, or thoughts, and insert comments after each part. The dream's "story" will unfold as you go.

Revealing the Secrets of a Dream

HERE'S AN ACTUAL DREAM that a friend asked me to help her interpret. Both she and her husband received a couple of dreams prior to this that seemed to indicate that they needed healing from some past wounds. She asked God for confirmation and direction, and as a result had the following dream. I've quoted the entire dream, including her comments. As you read it, you'll see how difficult it would be to interpret without first separating it into bite-size pieces. I've also included my comments in the interpretation:

The dreamer writes: I think I understand the reason I'm facing backwards (past?), and the back windows (seeing the past?)—but that's as far as I can decipher, so far...

I'm in the driver's seat of an old, full-size, pickup truck with a camper on the back. I'm parked in an old, dirt parking area on the peripherals of a restaurant, like an old "hamburger joint." (It's not a fancy restaurant.) There seems to be no other cars around this "outer area." I've volunteered to help two people, a husband and wife (I think), who need transportation for themselves and several cardboard boxes of their goods and possessions (not sure what those goods are). Their car has broken down, or something, and they're stuck... (I think they're like folks you sometimes see around here, coming from out of state trying to find work—everything packed in their old vehicle—just kind of indigent, desperate, and needy.)

The main theme seems to be that I am turned backwards in the driver's seat trying to uncover the backseat cab windows. It must be one of those trucks with a backseat in the cab.

The scene changes: Now the needy couple are in the truck's backseat. The back windows are covered with a cloth curtain on the back-passenger side, and some kind of canvas, like a window shade, on the driver's side. So, I'm on my knees faced backwards and I'm trying to pull the back, passenger-side, cloth curtain out of the way, so I can see while driving. I'm explaining all this to the couple in the backseat, as I struggle to tie the curtain back, and make it stay back out of the window. I spot my husband outside the truck (by the back-passenger window I'm struggling with), and ask him to come help me uncover the windows. I explain to him that it will be dangerous for me to drive this big truck, with the big camper on the back, if I can't see clearly. He then comes around the back of the truck to my side to help me. In the dream I'm thinking how dumb it is to have these window coverings for privacy there in the first place.

The next scene: We're all four outside the truck. We haven't gone anywhere and the couple's boxes are now being unloaded, while I watch. There's also no camper on the back of the truck anymore. The boxes are all empty—just empty cardboard boxes, heaped up! A young man comes running across the lot to unload these, for he says he wants the boxes. I look to see if I want to keep any of the empty boxes myself, before they're crushed and unusable, but none seem usable; just old used boxes, in varying colors, bent-up, etc. Then I wake up.

By reading the dream slowly and prayerfully, you can see just where to stop and insert the different thoughts that the symbols inspire within your heart. The dream reveals its mysterious secrets as you carefully examine and ponder each part of its message. It's like breaking and eating bread. You chew each bite thoroughly before swallowing.

I'm in the driver's seat of an old, full-size, pickup truck with a camper on the back.

Your truck is the work you're presently doing within yourself. You're the driver of your "old" truck (life). The camper on the back probably represents problems or troubles of your past that are covered (but not dealt with). It's the "load" you carry.

I'm parked in an old, dirt parking area on the peripherals of a restaurant, like an old "hamburger joint." (It's not a fancy restaurant.) There seems to be no other cars around this "outer area."

You're not going anywhere because God always stops us for "unloading" (healing). In addition, you're alone on the parking lot as this is not a "group" thing. God usually deals with each one of us personally and heals us privately.

I've volunteered to help two people, a husband and wife (I think), who need transportation for themselves and several cardboard boxes of their goods and possessions (not sure what those goods are). Their car has broken down, or something, and they're stuck... (I think they're like folks you sometimes see around here, coming from out of state trying to find work–everything packed in their old vehicle–just kind of indigent, desperate, and needy.)

Those two people represent you and your husband. You've "volunteered" through prayer to "aid" yourself and your husband. Everything packed in your old, broken-down vehicle indicates that you're desperate, despondent, poverty-stricken—in need of a Savior.

The main theme seems to be that I am turned backwards in the driver's seat trying to uncover the backseat cab windows. It must be one of those trucks with a backseat in the cab.

Your observation about the reason for being turned backwards in the seat is right on—you're trying to uncover your past.

Now the needy couple are in the truck's backseat. The back windows are covered with a cloth curtain on the back-passenger side, and some kind of canvas, like a window shade, on the driver's side. So, I'm on my knees faced backwards and I'm trying to pull the back, passenger-side, cloth curtain out of the way, so I can see while driving. I'm explaining all this to the couple in the backseat, as I struggle to tie the curtain back, and make it stay back out of the window.

Remember, what you're trying to uncover are old memories so that you can replace the wounds and bruises with useful wisdom. Being on your knees represents prayer. The curtain is your weapon of defense (self-justification or denial, including self-denial) to deflect the pain. Fear and pain are both curtains. (You need to push them out of the way to deal with your memories.)

I spot my husband outside the truck (by the back-passenger window I'm struggling with), and ask him to come help me uncover the windows. I explain to him that it will be dangerous for me to drive this big truck, with the big camper on the back, if I can't see clearly. He then comes around the back of the truck to my side to help me.

I think God is telling you that you should enlist your husband's help in this healing process. As you said before, God wants you to be healed and not get bogged down in the process. You no doubt will need his (or some counselor's) help.

In the dream I'm thinking how dumb it is to have these window coverings for privacy there in the first place.

Yes, they're very dumb. Defense mechanisms imprison us, enslave us, rob us, and deceive us into thinking that they're helping us!

We're all four outside the truck. We haven't gone anywhere and the couple's boxes are now being unloaded, while I watch. There's also no camper on the back of the truck anymore. The boxes are all empty—just empty cardboard boxes, heaped up!

This is the good part. No more covering, hiding, lugging useless junk around as you go forward. You just have to unload the boxes. And remember, those boxes and the things in them are nothing but old memories with their associated pains, offenses, etc.

A young man comes running across the lot to unload these, for he says he wants the boxes.

May I introduce *Jesus?*

I look to see if I want to keep any of the empty boxes myself, before they're crushed and unusable, but none seem usable; just old used boxes, in varying colors, bent-up, etc.

Give all those old memories to Him. You don't need to keep a single one. Those we keep are the ones we secretly want revenge or recompense for. So let Him have them all; they're not worth the space they take up in your heart!

Sweet Dreams!

Chapter Thirteen

Questions, Anyone?

To complete our discussion on dreams and their meanings, following are ten questions I've been commonly asked, along with valuable and informative answers:

1. When I have a dream, how do I know that it's from God?

In most cases, you will not know until you have correctly interpreted it. Once it's interpreted, if the message it contains agrees with the righteous principles found in the Bible, it's more than likely from Him. The Bible says, "All scripture [and I might add, 'every dream that's from God']...is profitable for doctrine, for reproof, for correction, for instruction in righteousness" (2 Tim. 3:16). If a dream's interpretation does not meet this test, I discount it. The dream itself may use language or symbols that are not in the Word; however, the correct interpretation will always conform to God's Word if the dream is from Him.

If we use our personal experience or our cultural perspective when interpreting dreams, we are subject to error. If we use any criteria other than God's Word to determine a dream's source, we are building on an incorrect foundation. The only valid test to decide whether a dream's message is from God is to ask yourself the same question you ask when determining if a doctrine is from God: "Does it agree with God's Word?" We should learn to discern and judge both doctrines and dreams.

The problem I've encountered in America is that our society has taught us that our dreams are nonsense. Therefore, we simply ignore them because there's nothing in the average dream to indicate that it's from God. There's no discernible anointing accompanying it. It's "just a dream." Most "anointed" dreams are actually "night visions," and need little or no interpretation. For the great majority of people, saints and sinners alike, the only real way of knowing if a dream is valid is to apply its message to the situation or life that it addresses, and then evaluate its value and purpose.

As I mentioned above, the actual content of a dream is not a valid test. The Bible says that God chooses the foolish things to confound the wise, so many very foolish and silly dreams are actually sealed messages from God:

> *For God speaketh once, yea twice, yet man perceiveth it not. In a dream, in a vision of the night, when deep sleep falleth upon men, in slumberings upon the bed; then he openeth the ears of men, and* **sealeth** *their instruction* (Job 33:14-16, emphasis added).

There is no better example than seven skinny cows eating seven fat cows (see Gen. 41:4). Talk about a pizza dream! Dreams are a lot like your mail. Without unsealing each envelope and reading each letter, there's no way of knowing just what each piece contains.

Because your own spirit can give you a dream, and it uses the same symbolism that God uses, it is necessary to "unseal" each dream before accepting or rejecting it. Jeremiah 29:8 says:

> *For thus saith the Lord of hosts, the God of Israel; Let not your prophets and your diviners, that be in the midst of you, deceive you, neither hearken to your dreams which ye cause to be dreamed.*

This Scripture informs us that all dreams aren't from God. If you want or fear something bad enough, you may dream about it. On the other hand, praying Christians need not fear receiving dreams from satan. Jesus said, "If a son shall ask bread of any of you that is a father, will he give him a stone? or if he ask a fish, will he for a fish give him a serpent?" (Lk. 11:11) When you ask God to communicate with you, He will not allow satan to answer for Him or He wouldn't be faithful to His own Word.

2. How can I know if I'm interpreting dreams the right way?

First, you should learn Jesus' method of interpreting parables, and Daniel's method of interpreting dreams. Follow their example. (Their methods are explained in my first book on dreams, *Understanding the Dreams You Dream*.) Afterwards, test your results. Your work with dreams should bring you into harmony with God and His purposes for your life. If it does that, you can bet that you're going about it in the right way.

3. If my children have dreams, can I assume that God is talking to them also?

Yes! You certainly can. Jesus said, "I thank Thee, O Father, Lord of heaven and earth, because Thou hast hid these things from the wise and prudent, *and hast revealed them unto babes*" (Mt. 11:25b, emphasis added).

It's wise to listen carefully when your children recite their dreams, because sometimes God uses them as His little messengers. You should treat their dreams like all others. Judge each dream's message by the Bible.

4. What does it mean when my child wakes up in the middle of the night crying from a bad dream?

There are several things that may cause "bad" dreams. If you and your husband have a disagreement in front of your children, you may frighten them and open their hearts to fear. If they've been traumatized at some point in their life, bad dreams may reveal they need counseling. On the other hand, some dreams are "body dreams." They are caused by things like pain. If you or your child has a stomachache, headache, or some other physical ailment, your dreams may be caused by your body's discomfort. Each case has to be judged on its own merits. In extreme cases, dreams may actually warn you of approaching calamity. There is no one single thing that causes bad dreams.

5. Since I really can't be positive about an interpretation unless I can apply it to the person or circumstance that it's about, are there some clues or something in each dream that will help me determine the subject matter it addresses?

Usually there are clues in every dream that reveal the subject. The very first part or scene of a dream presents the setting. By closely examining this first part, you can usually discern the dream's subject. If the dream has more than one scene, the first scene usually sets the stage for the play that follows. Each successive scene pertains to the same subject and carries the plot forward until the message is complete.

On rare occasions, you may wake up in the middle of a dream, then go back to sleep, and finish dreaming. If you do, pay close attention to the point where you woke up. If your dream is somewhat of a panoramic view involving your past, present, and future, the point in the dream where you woke up may indicate where you are in reality. In other words, the first part is your past and the second part is your present situation and possibly even your future. Remember, this isn't a hard and fast rule, because there could be other reasons your sleep was interrupted.

6. Is it normal to dream several dreams in one night?

Yes. It is not uncommon for some people to dream several dreams in one night, especially if God has a lot to say to them. On the other hand, if you dream several dreams and you don't wake up between them, they are all actually one dream. What appears to be several different dreams is actually different scenes from the same dream. Usually they are successive, but occasionally they're different views of the same thing.

7. Is it normal to dream several dreams in a row on successive nights, then go for several days or even weeks and not have a single dream that can be remembered?

Yes, it is normal. Sometimes prayer or even a fast may break the silence, but the absence of dreams is not uncommon at all. God doesn't seem to speak to anyone all the time. When He does speak, He has something important to say. Sometimes His apparent silence may have something to do with our lack of obedience in acting upon what He has already shared with us. In other words, why give us more when we haven't used what we've already been given?

8. I've dreamed several times that I lost my purse and was looking for it. What does that mean?

Your personal purse or wallet can represent something you treasure because of the valuables that you keep in it. It may also represent your heart. The two are closely related. Jesus said, "For where your treasure is, there will your heart be also" (Lk. 12:34). Your purse may also stand for your own identity.

9. What does it mean when one dreams about crows?

You'll find the answer to that question, and hundreds more like it, in my book, *Understanding the Dreams You Dream*. Besides a thorough discussion on how to interpret dreams, it contains a nine-part symbol dictionary that covers most of the things you dream about.

10. Is it possible to have the author come and conduct a seminar on interpreting dreams in our church?

Yes, your pastor can call or write me in order to schedule a program. You may want to give him a copy of this book and also a copy of *Understanding the Dreams You Dream*. He will then be familiar with my approach to dream interpretation and have an idea of what to expect from the seminar.

Other Books by Ira Milligan
E U R O C L Y D O N
Illustrating The Four Winds of Heaven

Euroclydon defines and illustrates the four winds of Heaven as they oppose the four winds of the earth (Dan. 7:2; Rev. 7:1). As the story of this ancient conflict unfolds, the role of the prophetic and apostolic ministries in the end-time Church is both clarified and explained. The restoration of the prophetic and apostolic ministries is part of God's end-time promise to *restore all things prophesied by the prophets from the beginning of time* (Acts 3:21). **Euroclydon** exposes and reveals several changes necessary before this promise can be realized.

The Anatomy of a *Scorpion*
Illustrating The Wheel of Nature

"Behold, I give unto you power to tread on serpents and scorpions, and over all the power of the enemy" (Luke 10:19). Most Christians know that *serpents* symbolize demons, but very few know the truth and power that lies hidden in the *scorpion's* symbolism. **The Anatomy of a Scorpion** unveils this mystery and reveals its practical application for every believer. A must for anyone interested in counseling and deliverance (price includes a counselors' aid: *The Wheel of Nature*).

Rightly Dividing the *Word*
Illustrating A Perfect Heart

One of God's favorite tactics to hide truth is to place it in plain sight, but disguise it as something other than what it is. Almost all spiritual truth is first clothed with a natural disguise. When we remove the natural covering, we find the naked truth! Like wheat, the natural husk must be removed from the grain before it is usable. An example of this is Moses' Law. The Law is spiritual, but it is clothed with various commandments and ordinances that hide its precious truths. These spiritual treasures are *"life unto those that find them, and health to all their flesh"* (Prov. 4:22). **Rightly Dividing the Word** carefully guides the serious Bible student step by step through the Scriptures to safely obtain these treasures.

To obtain a complete list of books and tapes available from Servant Ministries, Inc., complete and mail the information below. (Please print)

Name: _____

Address: _____

City: _____

State: _____ Zip: _____

Mail to: **Servant Ministries, Inc.**
P.O. Box 1120
Tioga, LA 71477

For information concerning having a seminar conducted in your church, contact Ira at: P.O. Box 1120, Tioga, LA 71477

Books On Dreams

UNDERSTANDING THE DREAMS YOU DREAM
by Ira Milligan

Have you ever had a dream in which you think God was speaking to you? Here is a practical guide from the Christian perspective, for understanding the symbolic language of dreams. Deliberately written without technical jargon, this book can be easily understood and used by everyone. Includes a complete dictionary of symbols.

ISBN 1-56043-284-5

UNDERSTANDING THE DREAMS YOU DREAM VOLUME 2
by Ira Milligan

Understanding the language God uses in dreams will open a whole new world of understanding His plan for each of us. Some dreams are directional, while some instruct us. Some will warn us, while others are the result of too much salsa on the taco! But how do you tell the difference? How do you know the meaning of things in your dream world? For instance, what do dragons or elevators mean? Is there significance in numbers, letters, houses, and water? *Understanding the Dreams you Dream Volume 2* offers answers to many questions. It can unlock the secrets to some of the most puzzling dreams. Most exciting, though, is the possibility that God's will and His divine blessing for you may be locked up within your dream world.

ISBN 0-7684-3030-5

DREAM INTERPRETATION
by Herman Riffel

Many believers read the scriptural accounts of dreams and never think it could happen to them. Today, though, many are realizing that God has never ceased using dreams and visions to guide, instruct, and warn. This book will give you a biblical understanding of dreams that you never had before!

ISBN 1-56043-122-9

DREAMS IN THE SPIRIT, VOL. 1
by Bart Druckenmiller

We all want to hear the word of the Lord. Nevertheless, many people don't. They limit how God speaks, not recognizing His voice throughout life's experiences, including dreams in the night and "daydreams" born of the Spirit. As a result, our lives lack vision and destiny. This book will introduce you to how God speaks through dreams and visions. It will give you hope that you, too, can learn to hear God's voice in your dreams and fulfill all that He speaks to you.

ISBN 1-56043-346-9

DREAMS IN THE SPIRIT, VOL. 2
by Bart Druckenmiller

This book encourages the present generation on the importance of dreams, which are divinely inspired and given by God concerning personal destiny. Dreams and visions are windows to the supernatural. Through them, God allows you to see beyond the natural into the realms of glory, where Heaven's decisions about your personal life, destiny, and ministry are made. In this book, the author teaches how to hold onto and fulfill the dreams and visions God gives you...plus much more!

ISBN 1-56043-347-7